To Holly Gail Atkinson
*We make the bearing point.*

# GOD REVISED

## How Religion Must Evolve in a Scientific Age

### GALEN GUENGERICH

palgrave
macmillan

First published in 2013 by
PALGRAVE MACMILLAN®
in the United States—a division of St. Martin's Press LLC,
175 Fifth Avenue, New York, NY 10010.

Where this book is distributed in the UK, Europe and the rest of the world,
this is by Palgrave Macmillan, a division of Macmillan Publishers Limited,
registered in England, company number 785998, of Houndmills,
Basingstoke, Hampshire RG21 6XS.

Palgrave Macmillan is the global academic imprint of the above companies
and has companies and representatives throughout the world.

Palgrave® and Macmillan® are registered trademarks in the United States,
the United Kingdom, Europe and other countries.

An excerpt appears from the poem "At the Smithville Methodist Church."
Copyright © 1986 by Stephen Dunn, from *New and Selected Poems, 1974–1994*
by Stephen Dunn. Used by permission of W. W. Norton & Company, Inc.

An excerpt appears from the poem "Family Reunion." Copyright © 2001 by
the University of Chicago, from *Bat Ode* by Judith Merrin. Used by permission
of the University of Chicago Press.

ISBN: 978–0–230–34225–5

Library of Congress Cataloging-in-Publication Data

Guengerich, Galen.
    God revised : how religion must evolve in a scientific age / Galen
  Guengerich.
      p. cm.
    Includes bibliographical references.
    ISBN 978–0–230–34225–5 (alk. paper)
    1. Religion—Philosophy. 2. Knowledge, Theory of (Religion) 3. God.
  4. Religion and science. I. Title.

BL51.G777 2013
211—dc23                                                    2012042049

A catalogue record of the book is available from the British Library.

Design by Newgen Imaging Systems (P) Ltd., Chennai, India.

First edition: May 2013

10 9 8 7 6 5 4 3 2 1

Printed in the United States of America.

# Contents

# Acknowledgments

When people ask me how long it takes to write a twenty-minute sermon, I sometimes say a lifetime—or however many years I happen to have lived at the time. The same principle holds true when asking how many people it takes to write a book, especially one with an expansive scope. It takes everyone: the human drama as it has unfolded since time began and continues today. So to everyone who made this book possible, I say thank you.

Nonetheless, some people merit special thanks, though I take full responsibility for the views I set forth and any errors that remain. I'm grateful to Nancy King Bernstein, Louise Brockett, Bernard Ferrari, Rob Hardies, Elisabeth Sifton, and Carole Sinclair for their early stage contributions to this project. I'm also grateful to John Baumgardner, Gary Dorrien, Welton Gaddy, Helio Fred Garcia, Alan Jones, Serene Jones, and Elizabeth Robinson, who made perceptive assessments of the initial proposal, and to Terasa Cooley, Gary Dorrien, and David McClean for their helpful comments on the initial manuscript.

Franklin I. Gamwell, who has been my intellectual mentor for twenty-five years, helped me refine the proposal and provided an especially careful reading of the initial manuscript. For his generosity of time and spirit, and for introducing me to the thought of Alfred North Whitehead, I will be forever grateful.

I could not imagine a more engaged and enthusiastic champion than my agent Jim Levine and his team at Levine Greenberg. And I've been continually inspired by the energy and vision of Karen Wolny and her team at Palgrave Macmillan. I'm deeply grateful for the steadfast support and encouragement that Jim and Karen have generously offered to me.

In significant measure, this book emerges from my ongoing twenty-year conversation with the members and friends of The Unitarian Church of All Souls in Manhattan, where I serve as senior minister. It's an extraordinary congregation filled with talented, engaged, and committed people. I've been moved by their openness, inspired by their honesty, and challenged by their aspiration. I feel blessed to live and minister among them. Special thanks are due to those who were willing to share their stories.

I'm also grateful for those who constitute the world of my Mennonite upbringing, and especially to my parents Twila and Owen Guengerich. Though they won't agree with some of the conclusions I have reached, their example continues to guide me, and their conviction that my work is important work strengthens my own commitment.

From where I now view the world, two people stand in the foreground: my daughter, Zoë Guengerich, and my wife, Holly Atkinson. I love them both without measure, and their encouragement of my work as a minister and writer remains indispensable. For me, Zoë is both symbol and substance of the reason that religion needs to evolve: to create a better world not only for ourselves, but also for succeeding generations—and especially for women.

Holly has been my steadfast champion throughout. She's my best friend and lover, as well as my essential partner in conversation and my first reader. Her unyielding resolve to transform the world continually inspires me. Alfred North Whitehead, who joined the faculty at Harvard at age 63, once said of his relationship to his wife Evelyn, "By myself I am only one more professor, but with Evelyn I am first-rate." I know how he felt, and why. Thank you, my love.

**CHAPTER 1**

# Where We Begin

## *From Mennonite to Manhattan*

The exquisitely beautiful summer Sunday afternoon brought the typically reclusive Amish out in droves. Buggies of all types—sober black sedans, gleaming courting buggies, and even a few swift sulkies—coursed along the winding roads of Lancaster County, Pennsylvania. Most moved along smartly, drawn by horses bound for a reward of water and oats. But the Amish passengers took their day of rest to heart. Dressed in colorful shirts and primly elegant dresses, they seemed relaxed, even jovial.

My daughter Zoë, then seventeen, and I had journeyed to Lancaster to visit Franklin & Marshall College (my alma mater) and to deepen her firsthand knowledge of my religious roots. Our route meandered through the lush patchwork farmland east of Lancaster. As our car slowed to a crawl behind a covered, sedan-type buggy, a water balloon all at once flew out of it, only to splash harmlessly against the side of an oncoming buggy. Moments later, the balloon thrower took aim with a more precise weapon. He unleashed his Super Soaker—the AK-47 of water guns—at a young couple in the approaching open-top courting buggy. The water found its unsuspecting marks, eliciting howls of protest from the couple and peals of laughter from inside the sedan buggy.

The idea of Amish people lazing on a Sunday afternoon, having fun with water weapons, seemed almost as incongruous as horse-drawn buggies on a paved road. The Super Soaker seemed incongruous as well, especially since we were just a few miles from the scene of the Nickel Mines Amish School shooting, where in October 2006 a gunman—Charles Carl Roberts IV, who was not Amish—shot ten Amish girls, killing five, before turning his weapon on himself. The Amish responded to that calamity with characteristic acceptance and self-effacing forgiveness. Along with the Mennonites, their somewhat more liberal religious first cousins, the Amish believe God calls them to be "the quiet in the land," set apart from the ways of the world. For most, this belief commits them to a life of austere conformity—except occasionally on a Sunday afternoon.

I was born on a dairy farm in a small Mennonite community in central Delaware. The Mennonites of my upbringing remain as robustly religious as Orthodox Jews and practicing Muslims. From the age of six weeks, Zoë grew up in Manhattan—perhaps as secular an environment as anywhere in the world. Our trip through the Lancaster countryside stemmed from my desire to show her how my journey from Mennonite to Manhattan began.

Present-day Mennonites range from the Amish-like Old Order Mennonites, who shun almost all the insights and conveniences of the modern world, to mainstream Mennonites, whose appearance and lifestyle conform to those of other Bible-centered, pacifist Christians, such as the Quakers and the Brethren. The middle ground is occupied by the Conservative Mennonites, who try to meet the modern world halfway. This was the faith of my upbringing. We had electricity, for example, but no television. We dressed in a manner that was two decades behind the times, not a century behind like the Amish. Our lifestyle was austere without being reactionary.

More than anything else, my life as a Mennonite was defined by a clear sense of the difference between us and them—between our community of faith and the rest of the world. I was first and foremost a Mennonite. Until my family moved to south Arkansas when I was nine years old, I recall no significant ongoing interaction with anyone who was not Mennonite. My friends, our neighbors, and my teachers and classmates at the Mennonite school I attended (two grades per classroom): all were Mennonite. I was also related to almost everyone I knew, or so it seemed to me.

The care and feeding of the Mennonite faith pervaded every aspect of my parents' lives, and mine as well. When I was two years old, my father was ordained to the Mennonite ministry in the red brick church where my maternal grandfather had long served as a minister. My father would not be the last in the ministerial line: six of my eleven uncles are (or were) also Mennonite ministers, along with twenty-five of my fifty-six first cousins or their spouses, at recent count.

When strangers ask me what I do for a living, I sometimes say that I'm in the family business. I too am a minister: now senior minister of All Souls Unitarian Church in New York City, one of the leading churches in the Unitarian Universalist denomination. My journey from Mennonite to Manhattan has taken me far from my roots—hence my interest in taking my daughter on a religious-history tour.

I showed her where I graduated from high school and where the Nickel Mines shooting had taken place. I showed her where the movie *Witness* had been filmed and where you can get the best shoofly pie on the planet. I showed her the little Mennonite church where, during part of my time as a classics student at F&M, I had served as acting pastor.

"Can you imagine me living here?" I asked.

"Yes," she responded, almost wistfully. "It's so beautiful, and orderly, and peaceful." Then she added, "I can also understand why you left."

Though I didn't press her at the time, my guess is that she sensed how I had reacted to the relentless emphasis on certainty and conformity. I felt claustrophobic. I needed more elbow room, in both my mind and my life. I sought freedom.

Like Orthodox Jews, Conservative Mennonites tend to live in relatively cloistered communities—and with good reason. The Mennonite tradition began in the wake of the Reformation, a brutal conflict in the sixteenth century that split the Christians of Western Europe into two opposing camps: Protestants—initially made up mainly of what became Lutherans and Presbyterians—and Catholics.

Not surprisingly, when Protestants weren't busy fighting Catholics, they were busy disagreeing among themselves. For example, most early Protestants believed a person's eternal fate had been predestined by God before creation. The Mennonites, who derive from a breakaway movement known as the Radical Reformation, believe an individual can choose whether or not to believe. For this reason, Mennonites baptize only adult believers, not infants whose fate has supposedly been sealed by God's predestined plan. The reformers who believed in adult baptism were collectively known as Anabaptists, a term that means to baptize again—an acknowledgment that the earliest Anabaptists had once been baptized as infants. Mennonites also believed in the complete separation of church and state, which for them meant not going to war on behalf of the government.

Adult baptism and pacifism were not popular beliefs in sixteenth-century Europe. In 1525, the Protestant-controlled City Council of Zurich, where the Anabaptist movement began, issued a decree that parents who failed to have their infants baptized within eight days after birth were to be arrested and banished. Within several years, belief in Anabaptism was made a capital crime—punishable by death—throughout much of Europe, in both Catholic and Protestant regions.

When I was a young boy, my grandmother Amelia often read me stories about how Mennonites in Europe had suffered and died for their faith. We'd sit in her living room, she in her rocking chair and me on the hassock alongside. Almost always, we'd each have a butterscotch candy, as if to sweeten the bitter tales.

The survivors of the vendetta against the Anabaptists had kept a chronicle, which eventually became an eleven-hundred-page encyclopedia of persecution titled *The Bloody Theatre or Martyrs Mirror*. My grandmother's favorite story—she read it often—tells of Dirk Willens, a sixteenth-century Mennonite in Holland, who risked being baptized as an adult believer, and even baptized others, in defiance of the ban.

One day in 1569, Willens learned that the police were about to arrest him in his home. He ran out the back door, but soon the officers came after him in pursuit. When Willens came to a frozen canal, he ventured onto the ice and managed to make his way across. But an officer who attempted to follow him broke through and was about to drown in the icy water. Seeing the officer's plight, Willens obeyed the biblical injunction to love even his enemies. He turned back and assisted the officer to safety.

Willens's reward? To be burned at the stake as an Anabaptist heretic. When Grandma came to the end of the story, she read it slowly, shaking her head: "A strong east wind blowing that day, the kindled fire was much driven away from the upper part of his body, as he stood at the stake; in consequence of which this good man suffered a lingering death" (pp. 741–742).

After she finished, Grandma and I sat in silence for a few minutes. She didn't need to press the point. Willens's example of selfless love was moral enough.

Years later in seminary, I read the story of Dietrich Bonhoeffer, a pacifist German pastor and theologian. A leader of the Confessing Church that stood firmly against Hitler, Bonhoeffer became part of a plot to assassinate Hitler, which ultimately cost Bonhoeffer his life. In the midst of the struggle against the terrors of fascism, Bonhoeffer developed a distinction between what he termed cheap and costly grace. Cheap grace, Bonhoeffer explains in his book *The Cost of Discipleship*, is a trivial form of superficial redemption, one not accompanied by a life of discipleship—grace without a cross to bear. Costly grace, in contrast, comes to individuals whose commitment permeates every aspect of their lives (pp. 41–46).

For early Mennonites, grace came at a high cost. For almost two hundred years, the Mennonites "oftentimes were not permitted to have permanent places of abode, and were driven about and hunted down like wild beasts, compelled to dwell in caves and mountains, and other

secluded places, hold their meetings in secret, and suffer every imagin-
able form of injustice and persecution" (*Martyrs Mirror*, p. 3). Several
countries sent out soldiers and executioners—numbering a thousand
strong in one case—whose sole task was to ferret out Anabaptists and
put them to death. On the whole, this persecution accomplished its
deadly purpose.

Eventually, most of the surviving Mennonites came to the United
States or Canada in search of religious liberty. Daniel Guengerich, my
great-great-great-grandfather, set sail from Germany with his extended
family on May 9, 1833, bound eventually for Iowa. In his diary, he
described the final hours of the seventy-two-day trip, which was easier
than many—only one passenger died en route—but was nonetheless
filled with storms and sickness: "On Sunday August 11th the pilot
came, then there was great joy on the ship among the people. At night
many stayed on deck. About midnight light towers were sighted on
the American coast. In the morning at daybreak we saw land on the
right and on the left. There was great rejoicing that we once more saw
land" (p. 33).

Like so many others who came to the New World, the Mennonites
longed for religious freedom—a place where they could believe in
accord with their conscience, worship in accord with their faith, and
live in accord with their calling. They arrived with a strong sense of
the commitments that defined them and made them unique. These
commitments had emerged from generations of living in the religious
equivalent of a storm shelter: a tightly controlled environment designed
to be impervious to danger. As long as the storm of persecution raged
on, everyone understood that rigid constraints were necessary for the
community to survive. But once the sun of religious liberty began to
shine, some people began to feel restless. These restless souls developed
a hankering for freedom to explore the outside world. In most Amish
and Conservative Mennonite communities, the austerity has long out-
lived the siege.

In her novel *A Complicated Kindness*, the Canadian writer Miriam Toews, also a former Mennonite, describes this hankering for freedom. The novel centers on the experience of Nomi Nickel, a sixteen-year-old Mennonite girl trapped in a small Mennonite town in western Canada called East Village. Nomi yearns to go to the other East Village—the one in New York—where she can hang out with Lou Reed and Marianne Faithfull. The problem is that Nomi's church, led by an uncle she calls "The Mouth of Darkness," tries to keep her on the path of righteousness by stifling her.

In a withering reverie, Nomi describes what Mennonite means to her.

> *We're Mennonites. As far as I know, we are the most embarrassing sub-sect of people to belong to if you're a teenager. Five hundred years ago in Europe a man named Menno Simons set off to do his own peculiar religious thing. . . . Imagine the least well-adjusted kid in your school starting a breakaway clique of people whose manifesto includes a ban on the media, dancing, smoking, temperate climates, movies, drinking, rock 'n' roll, having sex for fun, swimming, make-up, jewelry, playing pool, going to cities, or staying up past nine o'clock. That was Menno all over. Thanks a lot, Menno. (p. 5)*

Nomi goes on to explain that, by denying themselves the pleasures of this world, Mennonites believe they'll be first in line to enjoy the pleasures of the next world. As a teenager, however, Nomi says her concern isn't what happens after she dies, but rather how to endure the absence of life before death. She quips that "the town office building has a giant filing cabinet full of death certificates that say choked to death on his own anger or suffocated from unexpressed feelings of unhappiness" (p. 4).

As to life after death, Nomi describes a conversation she once had with her typing teacher about eternal life.

*He wanted me to define specifically what it was about the world that I*
*wanted to experience. Smoking, drinking, writhing on the dance floor*
*to the Rolling Stones? Not exactly, I told him, although I did think*
*highly of* Exile On Main Street. *Then what, he kept asking me.*
*Crime, drugs, promiscuity? No, I said, that wasn't it either. I couldn't*
*put my finger on it. I ended up saying stupid stuff like I just want to*
*be myself. I just want to do things without wondering if they're a sin*
*or not. I want to be free. I want to know what it's like to be forgiven*
*by another human being . . . and not have to wait around all my life*
*anxiously wondering if I'm an okay person or not and having to die*
*to find out. (p. 48)*

For myself, I know the feeling of almost suffocating in the narrow
confines of a theological storm cellar. Like Nomi, I was expected to
accept the doctrine, conform to the lifestyle, and take on the identity.
I struggled mightily to make it work, remaining a Mennonite through
my mid-twenties. But I finally realized that I did not fit the Mennonite
mold, which is why thirty years ago I left the Mennonite Church and
headed out on my own.

I was a student at Princeton Theological Seminary at the time,
ostensibly preparing to become a Mennonite minister. When I went
to Princeton (not a Mennonite seminary), many of my relatives feared
I would lose my faith. This did not happen. What I lost was someone
else's faith; what I began to seek was a faith of my own. I wanted to be
myself. I wanted freedom.

Like most people who have found the right place by leaving the
wrong one, I initially thought of freedom in terms of absence: no obligations, no constraints, and no commitments. I imagined the open road
and the solitary traveler, Walt Whitman and Henry David Thoreau.
I hummed Kris Kristofferson's haunting refrain, Janice Joplin's voice
echoing in my ear, "Freedom's just another word for nothing left
to lose."

After I left the Mennonites, however, I discovered that freedom from one way of life leads to a welter of choices about possible alternative ways of life. For me, the issue wasn't one of degree: I didn't leave in search of a religion that would allow me to expand my wardrobe and my music collection, though clothes and music provoked persistent conflict between my parents and me as I was growing up. Rather, I wanted a fundamentally different way of life, one that would make sense in the modern world.

One way to define the modern world, according to the philosopher Charles Taylor, is by describing how conditions of belief have changed. In his book *A Secular Age*, he points out that the shift to secularity in this sense consists of a change "from a society in which it was virtually impossible not to believe in God, to one in which faith, even for the staunchest believer, is one human possibility among others. I may find it inconceivable that I would abandon my faith, but there are others, including some possibly very close to me, whose way of living I cannot in all honesty just dismiss as depraved, or blind, or unworthy, who have no faith (at least not in God, or the transcendent). Belief in God is no longer axiomatic. There are alternatives" (p. 3).

Ours is a secular age not because God is absent from the world, but because we now have "a plurality of options" for understanding the purpose of our existence and creating meaning in our lives. Secularism is not about the elimination of religion, but about the proliferation of choices.

When I left the Mennonite Church in my mid-twenties, I had a choice to make. Initially, I threw out both the supernatural baby and the religious bathwater. I relished my freedom. I could read the newspaper—even watch television—on Sunday mornings instead of going to church. I didn't have to follow all the rules, and I didn't.

Over time, I came to realize that I needed to develop some rules of my own, some guidelines for what I thought it meant to live a good life. From where would these rules and guidelines come? I had rejected the authority of the Bible and the Mennonite Church, but I needed something more solid to base my life upon than whatever whim happened to capture my fancy at the moment.

I also began to miss the community of the church, the sense of being part of a larger group and working alongside others to achieve a larger purpose. I missed having close friends and shared commitments. Granted, I had rejected the particular commitments of the Mennonite Church. But why couldn't a similar group of people unite around a different set of shared commitments and work toward a different larger purpose?

Once outside the shelter of the Mennonite Church, I was able to sort out what I intended to leave behind from what I wished I could take with me. Over time, I discovered that my problem wasn't religion as a way of life; it was the idea of a supernatural God as creator, lawgiver, savior, and judge. The religions of the West—Judaism, Christianity, and Islam, along with their various permutations such as the Mennonites and the Amish—believe God exists above and beyond the realm of nature. In a word, they believe God is supernatural: able to command and control the forces of nature at whim (stop the sun, impregnate a virgin, and walk on water, to name three examples), in order to carry out the divine plan for creation.

If a supernatural God makes the rules and hands them down to humanity in the form of divine scripture, then religion becomes mere obedience in fancy clothes—or, if you're Amish or Mennonite, not-so-fancy clothes. Adherents to the three "religions of the book" believe God's revelation directs believers to obey God's commandments (Judaism), accept God's love in the form of divine salvation (Christianity), or submit to the will of Allah (Islam).

Here's the problem: the universe doesn't work that way. Half a millennium ago, a Polish astronomer named Nicolaus Copernicus peered into the night sky and made a discovery that fundamentally changed our understanding of the universe and our place in it. Through careful observation, Copernicus confirmed that the Sun, and not the Earth, occupies the center of our solar system.

In more recent times, scientists have made another discovery of similar magnitude: the laws of nature apply everywhere and always. In 1905, Albert Einstein articulated the theory of relativity, which applies to large-scale interactions among and within galaxies. During the first half of the twentieth century, a group of scientists (including Einstein) developed quantum mechanics, a branch of physics that describes interactions at the atomic and subatomic levels. It's too soon to tell whether superstring theory will fully reconcile relativity and quantum mechanics, but one thing is clear: these fundamental laws of nature have existed from the very beginning of our universe, they apply everywhere, at all times, and they do not change. The evidence now demands that the idea of a supernatural God, like the idea of an Earth-centered universe, must be revised. It should rapidly be relegated to the category of archaic relics.

Like the Amish buggy, the belief in a supernatural God is the lingering vestige of a bygone era. This belief may be quaintly appealing at times, but it's completely dysfunctional as the principal means of interpreting our modern world. Of course, the fact that buggies no longer make sense as our primary mode of transportation doesn't mean that we don't need vehicles. We have—and need—more vehicles than ever, including planes, trains, and automobiles.

In a similar way, the fact that God turns out not to be supernatural doesn't mean that God doesn't exist or that we don't need to participate in a religious community. In fact, our need for God and religion is greater today than it has ever been. If God is not supernatural, then religion has a serious role to play. Religion is the process of taking everything we know about the universe into account and creating a life of meaning and purpose within it. In order to play this new role, religion must continue to evolve, and our understanding of God must continue to evolve as well. The great religious challenge of our time is adapting our faith to the reality that God is not supernatural.

Religions have never been adept at accommodating fundamental change. It took five hundred years for the Roman Catholic Church to forgive Nicolaus Copernicus for looking into the night sky and reporting what he saw. Copernicus died of natural causes before the theological backlash against his discovery gained lethal momentum.

Two of Copernicus's scientific contemporaries, Giordano Bruno and Galileo, weren't so fortunate. They agreed with Copernicus that the Earth—and thus humanity—wasn't at the physical center of God's creation. Bruno dared to suggest that space is boundless and that the universe might be home to many solar systems; he was burned at the stake. Galileo was tortured, forced to recant the Copernican discovery, and spent the rest of his life under house arrest. In some parts of the world, modern-day truth-tellers suffer similar fates.

To be sure, there is a key difference between an Amish buggy and a supernatural God. The buggy was once a state-of-the-art mode of transportation. In our universe as we understand it, God was never supernatural, nor did the Sun ever revolve around the Earth. Like Copernicus, we need to adapt our understanding and way of living to accommodate this new reality.

How do I know God isn't supernatural, you may ask? As we will discuss in chapter four, there's no way to prove definitively that a supernatural God doesn't exist. It's theoretically possible to claim, as Deists do, that God created the universe and then, releasing creation to its own devices, went off to do other things. But as we shall see, there are no logical or empirical reasons to believe such a God exists, and there are plenty of compelling reasons to believe such a God does not.

Some people today, including many leading scientists, argue that if God isn't supernatural, then the idea of God and the purpose of religion are obsolete. This is sloppy logic: it would be like Bruno and Galileo declaring that if the Earth is not the center of the universe, then the universe doesn't exist. We certainly need to rearrange the theological constellations, but this doesn't mean the sky is empty. Our challenge is to integrate what we have learned about God into what we know about religion.

How long will it take for the religions of the West to make this shift? I hope that it won't take five hundred years. When I look at the physical and institutional violence being perpetrated today in the name of a supernatural God, especially against women and GLBT people, as well as against the Earth itself, I feel a deep urgency to help shift the paradigm. Blind fealty to the ancient dictates of a supposedly supernatural and decidedly male God has been wreaking havoc long enough. It's time for us to wake up, look up, and accept the truth about our universe and our lives.

If we don't, the practice of religion will become increasingly archaic: a horse-drawn buggy on a high-speed freeway. And yes, collisions will be increasingly frequent. This need not be the outcome, however. I believe religion can evolve in a way that addresses our ongoing need for meaning and purpose in the modern world.

Many people today agree that religion as currently practiced doesn't fully fit in the modern world. They grapple with the obvious tension between religion and science, between revelation and reason. According to the comprehensive US Religious Landscape Survey conducted by the Pew Forum on Religion & Public Life in 2008, 82 percent of Americans say religion is very or somewhat important in their lives. More than 90 percent believe in God or a universal spirit, 79 percent think miracles still occur today as in ancient times, and 66 percent view the sacred text of their religion as the word of God. Yet more than half of Americans believe evolution is the best explanation for the origins, or played a role in the development, of human life. Overall, 40 percent of Americans across all religious traditions see a natural conflict between being a devout religious person and living in a modern society.

For this reason, Americans as a whole find themselves religiously restless: nearly half of us, myself included, no longer belong to the tradition of our childhood faith. Most spiritual seekers try to diminish the dissonance we feel by joining a different faith tradition; a minority rejects religion altogether in favor of atheism. Whichever strategy we employ—stay put, make a change, or bail out—Americans of all persuasions are looking for a way to reconcile the consolations of faith with the certitudes of modern science.

It's certainly possible to believe that Jesus was the offspring of Mary and the Holy Ghost and yet choose to have an MRI to identify the cause of your lower back pain. This spiritual splitting between magic and science goes on all the time. But it requires trying to inhabit two incompatible universes at once. For my part, I don't believe this spiritual schizophrenia is necessary. There's a better way to be religious, and this book is my attempt to describe that better way.

Perhaps you agree, at least partly. Maybe you've already set aside in your mind the doctrines and dogmas you find hard to accept. Nonetheless, you find yourself drawn to a religious community where you find a sense of shared purpose and mutual support. Or maybe you've already abandoned religion altogether, driven out by the haunting specter of a judgmental God or the corrosive brutality of a harsh orthodoxy. Yet you may sometimes wonder whether, by avoiding the worst religion has to mete out, you've also deprived yourself of religion at its best: the experience of the sublime and the sacred, the celebration of beauty and the search for truth, the embrace of your deepest longings and the pursuit of your highest aspirations. However you experience the dissonance, my purpose is to show how you can resolve it—both in your mind and in your heart.

The resolution will come neither from science nor from religion alone—especially if religion continues to be defined as worship of a supernatural God, whose word launched creation and whose command must be obeyed. Ironically, both God's defenders and God's critics agree about the fundamental nature of religion as traditionally understood and practiced. They simply disagree about whether religion is true (and such a God exists) or false (and such a God does not exist). As one member of All Souls quipped about her husband, a badly lapsed Catholic: "He believes the Catholic Church is the one true church; it just happens to be false."

As a child of the age of science, I refuse to place blind faith in a scripture that contains obvious scientific and historical errors. I won't worship a God who clears parking spots for favored believers while allowing innocent children to be ravaged by cancer or swept away by a tsunami. Yet I also believe in a mystery that lies beyond human reason. There is more to the meaning of life than can be determined by using formulas and microscopes.

We need to move beyond the either/or dualism of the current battle between religion and science. We need a third option: an approach that begins with the scientific question of what we know about ourselves and our universe, and then moves—without magical thinking—to the religious question of what our knowledge means to us. This book charts this third way, one that partly agrees with the critics of traditional religion, who rightly insist that the supernatural God doesn't exist (and wrongly relegate religion to the dustbin of history), but also partly agrees with the defenders of traditional religion, who rightly insist that religion is a necessary dimension of human life (and wrongly cling to the idea of a supernatural creator and controller). In other words, both the critics and the defenders of traditional religion are 100 percent half right. Simply put, this book reconciles religion with the modern world.

We begin by asking about the source of our most certain knowledge: how do we know what we most truly know? We then tackle the daunting question of what it means to talk about God or worship God—if God is not the supernatural creator imagined by the religions of the book. And what about us as human beings: do we need to be saved? If so, from what? What is the human predicament that only religion can resolve? We'll also explore the purpose of faith, once freed from the mandate to believe in supernatural revelation. And we'll ask about religion: why it's necessary and what role it plays in constructing a life that is satisfying and meaningful.

The reason religion is necessary, after all, isn't so we can find salvation for the next life, but rather so we can find meaning and purpose in this one. We'll focus on gratitude—both as a spiritual discipline that continually reminds us of our dependence on the people and world around us, and as an ethical imperative that demands that we nurture the sources of our sustenance in return.

As we explore these matters together, we'll discover that religion is not mainly a set of beliefs. Rather, it is first and foremost a way of life. For this reason, the comprehensive religious question is not "What do you believe?" but rather "What do you do?" Our actions speak the only language that matters. If you want to know what we think is important, look at how we spend our time. If you want to know what we value, look at how we spend our money. If you want to know what we believe, look at how we live.

If I were to distill everything I know about religion and faith into a single dictum, it would be this: find your place in a religious community. It needs to be the right kind of religious community, of course. Not all religious beliefs are created equal. Some religious communities require people to believe things that aren't believable and to do things that aren't constructive. Some instill fear and foster bigotry, using religion to oppress and even destroy.

At its best, however, religion unites everything we know with everything we long for. The hallmark of a religious community is the experience of worship. By listening to transcendent music, we connect our hearts to the rhythm of eternity—to that sense of a nurturing presence we experience as divine. By pondering inspired readings, we connect our minds to the wisdom of the ages. In prayer, we proclaim our compassion for the brokenness in our hearts and in our world. In silence, we pour out our deepest longings to the Spirit of Life and Love. Through the ministry of the word, we declare our commitment to each other and our tenderness toward a needy world.

If you find the right kind of religious community, you have done the one necessary thing. You've found a place of solace for times of distress, a place of friendship when life feels lonely, a place of celebration when everything's grand. You've found a place where meaning and purpose fill the sanctuary and expand to fill your life.

As a child of science, I believe in religion. Which is why, on most Sunday mornings, you'll find me in church. And yes, the church is in Manhattan.

## CHAPTER 2

# How We Know

## *The Quest for Certainty*

In his 2012 keynote address to the annual South by Southwest music festival in Austin, Texas, the legendary New Jersey–born rock star Bruce Springsteen chronicled how pop music began and why it grew so rapidly. Once the domain of a few obscure southern blues players, this music coursed like lightning through popular culture during the 1950s and 1960s. By the time Springsteen came along, pop music was all the rage.

Why? Pop music became popular, Springsteen insisted, because of its power to transform expectations and experience. Starting with his own humble beginnings along the Jersey shore during the 1950s, he described how music from the little transistor radio atop the refrigerator gave voice to his innermost desires and frustrations.

In his address, Springsteen singled out the Animals, one of the most popular beat groups that came out of the 1960s. They appealed to him for two reasons: they were unattractive, and they were rebellious. The Animals had a reputation for being the ugliest band in music, which Springsteen—then in what he described as his hideous phase—found reassuring. And the Animals didn't care what anyone else thought about their looks, their music, or their way of life. As one of their signature songs puts it, "It's my life," and therefore no one can tell me what to do.

For Springsteen, the Animals held up a mirror to his feelings of being hideous and being held hostage. He wanted to escape the social and economic constraints of his upbringing in Freehold, New Jersey, a gritty, working-class town near the Jersey shore. In their song "We Gotta Get Out of This Place," the Animals gave voice to Springsteen's desperate longing for freedom. Their refrain became his refrain, too, and animated his quest to find a better life.

Springsteen did get out of Freehold. He found a better life. Springsteen went on to become one of the most influential songwriters and successful rock stars of the late twentieth and early twenty-first centuries.

I once had a transistor radio, too. Growing up Conservative Mennonite, I lived in a relatively cloistered environment: safe, secure, and insulated from the impact of the broader culture. We didn't have a television until after I left home, and the family radio was seldom on except once in a while to catch news headlines and the weather forecast.

When I was about twelve years old, I bought a transistor radio with money I had saved from mowing lawns and delivering newspapers. It was just the right size for illicit listening late at night under cover of blankets and a pillow.

The radio changed my world. While everyone else slept, I turned the dial, sampling various musical options. For the first year or two, I usually landed on a country music station. Two songs by Johnny Cash quickly became an obsession of mine. One was an anthem of alienated adolescence titled "What Is Truth?" Inexplicably, its refrain rang true for me too. During much of my youth, I felt more lonely than angry. But the question persisted: "What is truth?"

You would expect to hear such a cry at Woodstock in 1969 or at a college sit-in during the early 1970s. But why from a young Mennonite, especially one who should have known exactly what truth was? All my life I had been told precisely what truth was (the Word of God) and where I could find it (in the Bible).

The other essential Johnny Cash song was "Sunday Morning Coming Down," a Kris Kristofferson tune about someone waking up lonely on a city sidewalk one Sunday morning and wishing he hadn't prepared for the day by getting sober. Again, you can understand how this melancholy song would resonate with the experience of the homeless man who sometimes sleeps on a sidewalk grate alongside All

Souls in Manhattan. But why would it resonate with the experience of a twelve-year-old Mennonite boy who knew nothing about feeling lonely on a Sunday? That was the day we went to church and spent time with friends and extended family.

Nonetheless, I had to have these two songs. I knew my parents wouldn't let me buy the records on my own (this was in pre-iPod and even pre-CD days), but I also couldn't imagine going through life without them. I couldn't imagine growing old and not having ready access to "What Is Truth?" and "Sunday Morning Coming Down."

I cajoled my friend Bill, a Mennonite who was about five years older than me, into buying the records for me without telling my parents. Unfortunately, after the records were safely in my possession, Bill had a crisis of conscience and decided to tell. After a stern rebuke, my parents allowed me to keep the records anyway, perhaps because they saw the words "truth" and "Sunday" in the titles.

Over time, I recognized the source of my disenchantment with the faith of my upbringing: the relationship between "truth" and Sunday. The so-called truth I heard proclaimed in church on Sundays often contradicted the truth of my experience the other six days of the week. Tentatively at first, I began to question where our most certain knowledge comes from. I had always been told that it came from God—from God's Word as recorded in the Bible and interpreted by the church. But what happens when the supposed facts set forth in the Bible don't square with what we know to be true from experience—from observing how the world works?

You may have asked yourself the same question. You may have read some of the stories in the Bible—perhaps about God creating the world in less than a week, or God stopping the sun to give the Hebrews an edge in battle, or God impregnating the mother of Jesus. You've read some of the supposedly divine directives—to slaughter the infidels, for example, or kill the gays, or silence the women. And you've probably said to yourself: this doesn't seem divine at all. Someone must have made this up. When compared with other ancient literary texts, the Bible looks like a human document assembled for human purposes.

Or perhaps you haven't asked the question, at least not yet. Most people in ages past and many people today insist that divine revelation—God's Word as inscribed in scripture—contains our one reliable source of ultimate truth. If God supposedly said it, or inspired it, or authorized someone to say it, then we can have complete confidence in its ultimate truth because God is, well, God. If you are in this camp, I may not convince you otherwise by the end of this chapter. But please read on. And remember that the Bible's own testimony concerning its source and status can't be the deciding factor. The Bible's authority as divine revelation must be confirmed by some means other than the testimony of the Bible itself. When it comes to validating authority, "Because I said so" may be good enough for children, but it's not good enough for adults—and certainly not when ultimate truth is at stake.

This principle of external validation has been in place from the very beginning of the biblical tradition. Let's take another look at the iconic story of how the Ten Commandments came into being. As told in the Hebrew Bible, the people of Israel had been liberated from slavery in Egypt, and the prophet Moses had led them east into the wilderness, toward the mountain of Sinai. Three months after leaving Egypt, they pitched camp in the shadow of the mountain. According to the story, Moses told the people to prepare themselves for a meeting with God, which they did—for three days. The story continues:

*And it happened on the third day as it turned morning, that there was thunder and lightning and a heavy cloud on the mountain and the sound of the ram's horn, very strong, and all the people who were in the camp trembled. And Moses brought out the people toward God from the camp and they stationed themselves at the bottom of the mountain. And Mount Sinai was all in smoke because the Lord had come down on it in fire, and its smoke went up like smoke from a kiln, and the whole mountain trembled greatly . . . And the Lord came down on Mount Sinai, to the mountaintop, and the Lord called Moses to the mountaintop, and Moses went up . . . And God spake all these words, saying, "I am the Lord your God Who brought you out of the land of Egypt, out of the house of slaves. You shall have no other gods beside Me." (Exodus 19:16–20:3, excerpted; tr. Robert Alter)*

The rest of the commandments followed: don't worship idols or take God's name in vain; remember the Sabbath; honor your parents; and don't murder, commit adultery, steal, lie, or covet. That's it: ten commandments. When carved into stone, they became a visible symbol of the covenant between God and the people of Israel, as well as an enduring source of ethical guidance.

As a first draft of rules for living, the Ten Commandments are quite good. In fact, I object to the Ten Commandments being posted in courtrooms and classrooms across the nation not because I favor theft, adultery, and murder. Rather, I object to conveying the idea that the sole source of ultimate truth in the world is the God of smoke and fire on Sinai.

According to the story, the people of Israel had no such objection. Why? They accepted the commandments as authentic not because God said "I am the Lord thy God," but because of the thunder and lightning, the heavy cloud and the sound of the ram's horn, the fire and smoke, and the violent trembling. They believed the forces of nature were harbingers of God's presence. The divine commandments were believed to be true because nature provided an external validation.

If we assess the truth of the Bible today based on the same criterion, what do we find? Does our experience validate the Bible as the ultimate source of truth or call its traditional status as divine revelation into question? As we will discover, the question comes down to which comes first, belief or knowledge. Put more precisely, we'll ask whether belief is a subset of knowledge, or knowledge is a subset of belief.

The story of how we know what we know and why we believe what we believe is a fascinating tale, but it's not without complexity. After all, we are grappling with the fundamental assumptions of Western philosophy and religion. If this story were easy to tell and the challenges simple to resolve, I wouldn't have written this book, because the God Wars would already be over.

If you occasionally find the going hard in the pages ahead, I urge you to persevere. This chapter is where, as Robert Frost memorably puts it, two roads diverge—two radically different ways of understanding our lives and our world. And which road we take will, as Frost goes on to say, make all the difference. Everything is at stake in our discussion of how we come to know whatever it is that we know. So let's take to the road.

First, let's ask about our ordinary, day-to-day knowledge and what it typically means when we say something is true. In his memorably simple statement on the matter, Aristotle said that "to say that what is is, and what is not is not, is true" (*Metaphysics* [4.7.1]).

Fair enough. But, as President Bill Clinton not so memorably put it when trying to prevaricate his way out of responsibility for his affair with Monica Lewinsky, the truth depends on what you mean by "is."

When we say something is true, we usually mean that the purportedly true facts correspond to some attribute or property of the world beyond the statement itself. A true statement has a foundation—a basis—not just in language, but in life.

If I tell you that the sky is blue, for example, I'm saying that in the world of our experience, there is something we both know to be sky and, furthermore, that it's the color we both know to be blue. The blue sky isn't a figment of my imagination, nor is my saying that the sky is blue or the blue sky itself a figment of yours. Nor are you and I, along with the blue sky, a figment of someone else's imagination. If the statement is true, then we have reason to believe that, in actual fact, the sky is blue. Epistemologists (people who study what we know and how we know it) call this means of authenticating knowledge empirical foundationalism. The word "empirical" derives from an ancient Greek word that means "experience." We know something to be true because our experience gives us a basis—a foundation—for saying it's true.

There are also statements that we believe to be true because they have to be true. If I tell you that two parallel lines will never meet, you know that I'm telling the truth because two lines that never meet are, by definition, parallel. Epistemologists call this kind of truth-telling rational foundationalism. We know something to be true because logic says it has to be—even if we've never actually seen two parallel lines or verified that they never meet, which we haven't, at least not by experience. Nonetheless, we have good reason to believe that two parallel lines will never meet. If they did, they wouldn't be parallel.

But what if our mind is playing a trick on us when we think we see a blue sky or think we're thinking about parallel lines? Sometimes our experience sends us off on a wild goose chase. You may recall Scrooge's initial response when the ghost of Jacob Marley makes its appearance in Charles Dickens's *A Christmas Carol*.

"You don't believe in me," the ghost says to Scrooge.

"I don't," Scrooge replies.

"Why do you doubt your senses?" the ghost asks.

Scrooge responds, "Because a little thing affects them. A slight disorder of the stomach makes them cheats. You may be an undigested bit of beef, a blot of mustard, a crumb of cheese, a fragment of an underdone potato. There's more of gravy than of grave about you, whatever you are!" (p. 18).

The acknowledged champion doubter-of-senses, and in many ways the person who invented the sport, was the early sixteenth-century philosopher René Descartes. The prevailing view of knowledge at the time was an early version of what we today call empirical foundationalism.

Based on Aristotle, endorsed by the famed fourth-century theologian Augustine of Hippo, and incorporated into a school of thought known as Scholasticism by the equally famous thirteenth-century theologian Thomas Aquinas, this view of knowledge highlighted sense experience as our primary way of knowing.

Like Scrooge, Descartes knew that we can sometimes be mistaken about the content of our sense experience. In his *Meditations on First Philosophy*, Descartes's goal was to discover a foundation for knowledge that was doubt-proof, a foundation based on reason rather than sense experience. After careful thought about the matter, Descartes realized that he could doubt anything—except the fact that he was the one who was doubting. If he stood and looked at a tree, for example, he could find reasons to doubt that the tree was actually there. But he couldn't doubt the fact that the one who doubted—Descartes himself—was, in fact, doubting and therefore existed. Hence Descartes's conclusion, which he stated later in his *Principles of Philosophy* in its now-famous form: *Cogito ergo sum*. I think, therefore I am.

Descartes's goal was to shift the foundation of knowledge from the quicksand of sense experience onto the solid rock of reason. Because of his relative success in this effort, Descartes is often credited with developing rational foundationalism. But his approach to knowledge, insisting that we doubt everything we can, contributed to the development of a third approach to knowledge known as skepticism. If you can doubt that the tree you apparently see is actually there, why can't you also doubt that doubting is what you are actually doing or that you are the one doing it?

Taken to its logical extreme, skepticism eventually becomes solipsism, the view that my own mind is the only thing that I can know to exist. Everything else—my thoughts and feelings, other people's minds and experiences, the outside world—might be an illusion created by my own mind. This is what philosophers sometimes call the egocentric predicament.

While I don't believe solipsism or even skepticism has the final word when it comes to knowledge, the possibility that we might be mistaken about what we think we know is real. We should take the egocentric predicament seriously.

In his book *This Is Water*, the late novelist David Foster Wallace relates a parable. "There are these two young fish swimming along and they happen to meet an older fish swimming the other way, who nods at them and says, 'Morning, boys. How's the water?' And the two young fish swim on for a bit, and then eventually one of them looks over at the other and goes, 'What the hell is water?'" (pp. 3–4).

The point of this story, Wallace goes on to explain, is that the most important realities are often the hardest ones to see. Each of us is like a fish in water: there is no experience we've had that we were not the absolute center of. We also swim in the water we swim in, making it hard—even impossible—for us to see other rivers, lakes, and oceans, in which other fish swim in different waters. With our limited perspective as individuals, what seems true to us may not seem true to other people.

If I look out my office window onto Lexington Avenue one day, for example, and report that I see a lavender, sanctuary-sized turnip beckoning me to jump out my window, my colleagues at All Souls will rightly haul me off for psychiatric examination. Then again, if we discover that one of the balloons in Macy's Thanksgiving Day parade has gone rogue, my sanity will be saved—though we'd need to check to see whether the parade balloons have diversified into vegetables.

On the other hand, if billions of people over thousands of years look into the sky and see a near-circling orb pass through the heavens each day and night, and its movements are calculated to the last second, and eventually we send a probe into the heavens to collect a sample of it and then land people on its surface to walk on it, the chances are good that the moon is real. We instinctively trust our minds and our senses, especially when other people corroborate what we know.

In his book *What Does It All Mean?*, Thomas Nagel, a leading contemporary American philosopher, acknowledges that skepticism is hard to dismiss and impossible to refute. Yet, Nagel says, "I have to admit that it is practically impossible to believe seriously that all the things in the world around you might not really exist. Our acceptance of the external world is instinctive and powerful: we cannot get rid of it by philosophical arguments. Not only do we go on acting *as if* other people and things exist: we *believe* that they do, even after we've gone through the arguments which appear to show we have no grounds for belief" (p. 17).

If foundations are hard to establish and skepticism is hard to stomach, where do we turn? The Austrian philosopher Ludwig Wittgenstein, one of the leading philosophers of the twentieth century, offers a mediating option in his *Philosophical Investigations*. For Wittgenstein, the truth of a statement lies not in the foundational realities—whether ideas or experiences—to which the words themselves refer. Rather, its truth lies in the statement's power to make things happen and get things done. He likens language to a game, a language game.

In using language, Wittgenstein explains, one party calls out the words, the other acts on them. These acts may be physical actions, as when a builder tells an assistant to put this beam on that pillar. In response, the assistant does not define the word "beam" or the word "pillar," but indeed puts the beam on the pillar. To do anything else would be to play the language game by the wrong set of rules (para. 1–6).

What makes a statement true, Wittgenstein insists, is its ability to translate language into life: "To imagine a language means to imagine a form of life" (para. 19). This means, of course, that a statement may be true in one situation—one language game or one form of life—and not in another. For Wittgenstein, the question of whether and how a statement corresponds to a reality beyond the language game is the wrong question.

But that is precisely the question we are trying to ask. I'm not interested in whether, if people actually believe that the Bible is the one authoritative revelation of the one true God, they are able to understand their purpose in life and plan their days. As a language game, the Bible is one of the longest running and best performing. The question is whether, based on everything else we know about the world, the Bible is true beyond the world of the Bible and those who believe in it.

In epistemological terms, my interest in the basis of the Bible's claim to truth makes me an epistemological foundationalist, I suppose—and probably of both types, empirical and rational. I want to know the truth: what's logically true and what's true to life. My guess is that most people want the same. Some members of my congregation are fond of saying that they like coming to All Souls in part because they don't have to check their brains at the door of the sanctuary.

My own conviction is that we want to know what is foundationally true because we were born that way. In his book *Think: A Compelling Introduction to Philosophy*, the contemporary British philosopher Simon Blackburn corroborates this view. He writes, "We might thus suppose that evolution, which is presumably responsible for the fact that we have our senses and our reasoning capacities, would not have selected for them (in the shape in which we have them) had they not *worked*. If our eyesight, for example, did not inform us of predators, food, or mates just when predators, food, and mates are about, it would be of no use to us. So it is built to get these things right. The harmony between our minds and the world is due to the fact that the world is responsible for our minds. Their function is to represent it so we can meet our needs; if they were built to represent it in any way other than the true way, we could not survive" (p. 43).

The harmony between our minds and the world gets disrupted, however, when we are asked to believe things that our reason and sense experience tell us can't be true. Under these circumstances, what does it mean to get things right? More to the point, we need to ask whether religious belief operates under a different set of rules than our beliefs about other things.

Historically, the answer to this question has been yes. For most believers in the religions of the book, and especially for those who take their scriptures and creeds at face value, belief is a necessary prerequisite to understanding the natural world and human history. As Augustine famously exhorted in the fourth century: "For understanding is the reward of faith. Therefore do not seek to understand in order to believe, but believe that thou mayest understand; since, 'except ye believe, ye shall not understand'" (*Tractate 29 on John 7:14–18*).

Let's be clear about what this means. For Augustine, the Bible was the window through which he viewed everything else. In terms of our modern approach to describing knowledge, the Bible provided the foundation upon which both reason and sense experience rested. If the Bible says that Jesus raised Lazarus from the dead, we have to adjust what logic and experience tell us is possible in order to accommodate the more foundational "fact" that, according to the Bible, Jesus actually raised Lazarus from the dead.

Augustine's view held sway for more than a thousand years. Most people during this period—the Middle Ages—couldn't even read the Bible, which allowed the church to wield monolithic authority on questions of what people should believe and how they could be saved. This stranglehold began to weaken during the philosophical awakening we now call the Renaissance and the religious revolution we call the Reformation.

The Renaissance was a rebirth of interest in the philosophy and literature of ancient Greece and Rome. It began in the twelfth century but gained impetus in the fifteenth century with the rise of prosperity (more peace, less famine and plague) and the development of the printing press. When Constantinople fell in 1453, many Eastern scholars fled to Italy, taking with them important manuscripts and a tradition of

Greek scholarship. This source of knowledge presented the Europeans with an alternative to the religious orthodoxy that had prevailed for more than a millennium.

The Renaissance thinkers, like the Greeks two thousand years before, began to champion the individual as an instrument of reason and a source of knowledge. Eventually, this rediscovery of the individual sparked a religious revolt. In 1517, a German monk named Martin Luther nailed his list of ninety-five theses—his protest against rampant abuses in the Roman Catholic Church, especially the sale of indulgences—on the door of the church in Wittenberg, Germany. His critique started what came to be called the Protestant Reformation. In an incisive theological move, Luther charted a new path to salvation.

For centuries, the church had insisted that only priests could read and understand the Bible and that the sacraments of the church were the only means by which sinners could receive saving grace. The church also said that priests played an essential role in confession and the forgiveness of sin, and that the labor of penance, as required by the church, was necessary for salvation.

Luther rejected these requirements. He believed that salvation was a matter of God's spirit reaching out to an individual sinner, who responded in faith to God's offer of grace. Faith alone was sufficient, according to Luther. No confession to the priest was required, no sacraments necessary, no costly indulgence, no ritual of penance. Some of these elements had a place in the life of faith, but they were not needed for salvation. Salvation was a matter between God and the individual.

Over time, this paradigm shift would occur not only in religion, but also in politics (as democracy) and economics (as capitalism). Individual believers (and citizens and workers) had much to gain from these changes. For believers, however, the time would eventually come when they would be forced to decide which took precedence: belief in the revelation of a supposedly supernatural God or knowledge gained from reason and sense experience.

In the early 1930s, the American philosopher John Dewey gave a series of lectures at Yale that formed the basis of his book *A Common Faith*. Dewey begins with an eerily prescient remark: "Never before in history has mankind been so much of two minds, so divided into two camps, as it is today" (p. 1).

Dewey had in mind the battle between, as he put it, those who think nothing religious is possible apart from the supernatural, and those who think advances in culture and science have completely discredited the supernatural and all religions based on belief in it. Both camps, Dewey observed, equate religion with an unseen supernatural power that has control of human destiny and is thus entitled to obedience, reverence, and worship. As long as this view is held by both camps, he concluded, the conflict between science and religion will become increasingly protracted.

The real issue, according to Dewey, is not what facts we believe, but how we discover and justify our beliefs. Dewey divided the world between those who employ what he called the method of doctrine and those who employ what he called the method of intelligence. Doctrine is a body of fixed beliefs that must merely be taught and learned as true; the method of doctrine, therefore, remains closed to new insights. The method of intelligence, on the other hand, embraces an ongoing process of inquiry and discovery, open to new insights and accessible to everyone (pp. 1–4).

Today, we face the same dilemma. Which comes first, belief or understanding? Which method do we employ, doctrine or intelligence? Both Augustine and Dewey grappled with the same question, but they reached opposite conclusions. For my part, I ultimately sided with Dewey, though Dewey himself needlessly limited the method of intelligence to the scientific method, which he once called the only road to truth. Applied more generally, the method of intelligence yields knowledge and understanding; after taking into account everything I know, I can then decide what to believe. In siding with

Dewey, I rejected the Bible as the authoritative revelation of the one true God.

Make no mistake: I came to this conclusion slowly and hesitantly. I struggled with a persistently nagging question: what if I'm wrong? Read the book of Deuteronomy in the Old Testament sometime, or the book of Revelation in the New Testament. Would you want to get on the wrong side of a God who advocates dashing children against rocks and banishes the wicked to eternal torment? For months—truth be told, maybe years—I would lie awake at night calculating the odds that I was wrong. Eternity's a long time to wish you'd come to a different conclusion.

I kept running through the evidence, both rational and empirical. Rationally, I knew that the claim that God was all-powerful didn't make sense. If God could stop the sun, or impregnate a virgin, or raise someone from the dead, then the laws of nature weren't laws after all. They were temporary patterns, subject to change without notice.

Belief in divine revelation also means that we can experience the world around us, but we shouldn't base our knowledge upon it. If the creeds are to be believed, the so-called knowledge we glean from studying the Bible trumps both our reason and our experience. In the cold light of day, my conclusion seemed sensible and right, but alone at night, I would sometimes wonder: what if I'm wrong?

My doubts have dissipated over the years as I've learned more about both the Bible and the world. Biblical scholars have confirmed what even a casual reader of the Bible soon discovers: the Bible is internally inconsistent and historically inaccurate. Do these shortcomings make the Bible useless? Not at all: they make it literature, like Homer's *Iliad* or Euripides's *Bacchae*. The Bible reveals humanity at its worst and occasionally at its best. In that sense, the Bible contains inspiration and even wisdom—but only insofar as it dovetails with everything else we know.

The story of how the New Testament took shape over the first couple of centuries after the death of Jesus is a fascinating tale, especially as told by Bart Ehrman, one of the leading contemporary New Testament scholars. Raised an evangelical Christian, Ehrman studied the Bible intensively over several decades and eventually concluded that the Bible isn't what Christians claim it is. The New Testament contains a mélange of history and hijinks: the story of how Jesus, an apocalyptic prophet who believed the world would surely end within the lifetime of his disciples, became a literary puppet of ecclesiastical intrigue and political power.

Bottom line? The New Testament is a codex compiled by human beings—men, to be precise—for human purposes. As with any human endeavor, the use of lawyers, guns, and money to serve economic and political purposes rapidly comes to the fore in the story.

When members of my congregation show interest in this story, I sometimes suggest that they watch the movie *The Da Vinci Code*, based on Dan Brown's novel of the same title, and then read Ehrman's book *Truth and Fiction in "The Da Vinci Code."* I also suggest his book *Forged*, in which he argues that some of the books in the New Testament are anti-Jewish tracts covertly written by Christians but attributed to Jewish authors.

Biblical literalists protest these assertions. For them, faith is the willingness to believe that the Bible is an authoritative revelation of the one true God—despite ample evidence to the contrary. They insist that biblical inaccuracies and inconsistencies reveal a divine, rather than a human, origin. They insist that God intended the Bible to be hard to believe in order to test our faith.

This view of faith is nearly impossible to refute. It locates faith in the realm of the absurd, where the fact that something is impossible to believe makes believing it necessary and somehow therefore makes the belief itself true. Circular logic of this kind effectively inoculates faith against evidence.

The recent discovery of Ida, a 47-million-year-old primate, provides a case in point. Many scientists believe Ida provides a missing link between primates, who have opposable thumbs, and reptiles, which have long tails. Based on everything else we know, this fossil looks like what we expected someday to find, but never had—until now. It confirms the scientific method and empirical and rational approaches to knowledge.

For biblical literalists, this fossil is another opportunity to strengthen their faith in biblical doctrine. The fossil appears to be old—but only because, when God created the world 6,000 years ago, God made lots of things appear to be much older than they are, in order to test the faith of those who read the Bible.

The Institute for Creation Research, a fountainhead of biblical literalism, sets the benchmark for the method of doctrine. Writing to repudiate "Old-Earth Creationism," Henry Morris declares: "It all seems to us to hinge on one overriding question. Do we really believe the Bible to be God's inerrant Word or not? If the Bible is really the Word of our Creator God, then—by definition—it must be inerrant and authoritative on every subject with which it deals. This assumption leads clearly to the conviction that the creation took place in six literal days several thousand years ago. We believe this simply because God said so and said it quite plainly!" (http://www.icr.org/article/4535/).

The problem here isn't that the Bible makes assertions that we can't confirm using other sources of knowledge. It's that the Bible makes assertions for which we have clear counterfactual evidence: evidence that the claims are not true. The only reason to discount this evidence and disregard experience would be that a different set of so-called facts takes precedence. For many people today, it does. For biblical literalists, revelation trumps reason. The facts of experience simply don't matter.

Once we get into the habit of ignoring evidence, what's to stop us from an infinite regress to solipsism, in which the universe collapses into the human brain? In *Think*, Blackburn cites the observation of the famously skeptical philosopher Bertrand Russell, who asks, as

Blackburn puts it, "How do I know that the world did not come into existence a very few moments ago, but complete with delusive traces of a much greater age? These traces would include, of course, the modifications of the brain that give us what we take to be memories." Russell concludes, in Blackburn's words, "If you are skeptical about time, you quickly become skeptical about everything" (p. 46).

To be fair, many Christians take a dim view of creationism, insisting that the book of Genesis isn't meant to be read scientifically. But what about, say, the virgin birth and the resurrection of Jesus? When the testimony of the Bible contradicts what we conclude from the rest of our experience, we need to choose which takes precedence as the source of our most certain knowledge. For me, the choice is clear.

I recognize that some modern and postmodern theologians attempt to distinguish between how the Christian faith was originally articulated and how the Christian faith might best be formulated today. In other words, these theologians distinguish between what was said and what was meant, which allows the underlying meaning of a text to remain open to interpretations that suit our contemporary situation. To the extent that these efforts sidestep my critique of God as supernatural and the Bible as God's authoritative revelation, the resulting views would surely not be embraced by most Christians today as Christian. In any event, my critique focuses on the Christian faith as articulated by the primary Christian creeds and as understood by most Christian believers.

Make no mistake: I'm not saying that we shouldn't believe in God or that the Bible isn't an important work of wisdom literature. I'm simply saying that God isn't supernatural and that the Bible is not the ultimate authority on every subject with which it deals. The claim that the Bible is the authoritative revelation of the one true God has no logical foundation.

Nor does the claim have a convincing empirical foundation. Thirty years ago, I left the Mennonite Church—the faith of my upbringing and still the faith of my parents and much of my extended family—because I was forced to choose between the facts of human experience and the supposed facts of divine revelation. I could no longer ignore the overwhelming evidence that the religions of the book have wreaked needless havoc throughout human history. Crusades, Inquisitions, Wars of Religion, Witch Hunts, and Holocausts: the biblical religions have continually and persistently aided and abetted the most horrific human savagery—against infidels, of course, but also against gays and against women. The geographical location where the Venn diagram of the biblical traditions overlaps—the ancient city of Jerusalem—is arguably the single most blood-soaked square kilometer in the world. Given the actual historical evidence of how believers in the one true God have conducted themselves, I could no longer count myself one of them. Nor could I accept the biblically mandated subordination of women as a fact that made sense in the world as I experienced it.

The biblical position on women—the issue that ultimately spurred my departure—couldn't be clearer. As the Apostle Paul states in his letter to the Ephesians: "Wives, be subject to your husbands as you are to the Lord. For the husband is the head of the wife just as Christ is the head of the church, the body of which he is the Savior. Just as the church is subject to Christ, so also wives ought to be, in everything, to their husbands" (5:22–24. Unless otherwise indicated, all biblical quotes are taken from the New Revised Standard Version).

If you think the literal interpretation of this injunction has fallen out of favor, you would be wrong. Read Kathryn Joyce's book *Quiverfull: Inside the Christian Patriarchy Movement*. Joyce details how the biblical submission mandate forms the core belief of Quiverfull, an organization whose members insist that family planning of any kind—not only abortion, but contraception as well—is immoral and that women must accept every child as an unconditional blessing. Quiverfull takes its name from the verse in the Hebrew Bible that says, "Sons are indeed a heritage from the Lord, the fruit of the womb a reward. Like arrows in the hand of a warrior are the sons of one's youth. Happy is the man who has his quiver full of them" (Psalm 127:3–5).

The goal of the Christian patriarchy movement, as stated in their 200-year plan, is to win the culture wars through reproductive means: by reproducing more than other social groups, especially liberal-minded ones. The specifics of their plan were drafted and approved at a 2008 conference hosted by Vision Forum, the leading publisher of Christian home-schooling curricula (Joyce, pp. 229–231). Not surprisingly, daughters are controlled in this environment as tightly as wives. As one proponent put it, "If you have to boil courtship down to a sentence, it involves getting Dad involved and getting Cupid out of the picture" (Joyce, p. 231).

Quiverfull may be more extreme than many who champion the subjugation of women, but only by degree. As Joyce notes, the doctrine of submission remains official policy of the 16-million-member Southern Baptist Convention. Albert Mohler, the president of the Southern Baptist Theological Seminary, describes what is at stake for biblical literalists: "We must choose between two unavoidable options: either the Bible is affirmed as the inerrant and infallible Word of God, and thus presents a comprehensive vision of true humanity in both unity and diversity, or we must claim that the Bible is, to one extent or another, compromised and warped by a patriarchal and male-dominated bias that must be overcome in the name of humanity. For biblical traditionalists, the choice is clear" (Joyce, p. 16).

Mohler states the issue precisely. Either the Bible is the authoritative revelation of the one true God, or the Bible is a creature of its context. Most efforts to subjugate women around the globe are justified by the belief that scripture, whether Jewish, Christian, or Muslim, is an authoritative revelation from a supernatural God. In this view, scripture trumps everything else, including reason and experience.

I'll take Mohler's other option: the Bible is a creature of its context. Why have the religions of the book been so incorrigibly hostile to women? Because misogyny was in the water when these religions developed. Most non-biblical religious traditions also relegate women to a subordinate role. In historical terms, patriarchy preceded the gender of God. Because men put the tradition together, God turned out to be male, as did Moses, Jesus, and Mohammed—not to mention almost all of the rabbis, popes, priests, and imams in history. Only in recent years, and only in the liberal-most fringes of the Jewish and Christian traditions, have these patterns begun to change, and then only with great difficulty and controversy. As Mary Daly states in her prophetic 1973 book *Beyond God the Father*, "if God is male, then the male is God" (p. 19). Making the same point less succinctly and more comprehensively, Daly says, "If God in 'his' heaven is a father ruling 'his' people, then it is in the 'nature' of things and according to divine plan and the order of the universe that society be male-dominated" (p. 13).

Because this pattern of male behavior has been deeply embedded in the religions of the book, contemporary religious crusades remain just as vicious and destructive as the crusades of old. Fundamentalist Muslim women who venture outside their homes unaccompanied in Afghanistan fear for their lives, and fundamentalist Christian women in the United States find themselves banished to the kitchen and the nursery. Ultra-Orthodox Jewish women in Israel, not to mention Orthodox Jewish women in some parts of the United States, can't worship alongside their husbands and sons, and there's a move afoot to resegregate buses and shops in some Israeli communities by gender. If medical and technological advances had proceeded at the same pace as religious enlightenment over the centuries, we'd still practice bloodletting and communicate by smoke signal.

I simply cannot believe that, sixty years after the landmark signing of the Universal Declaration of Human Rights, people are still trying to subordinate women on religious grounds. How can this be? We've managed to discover a Higgs boson–like particle on the scantest possible evidence, but most believers haven't yet concluded, based on the largest possible sample size, that women deserve equal standing in every respect. Religious people should be leading the fight for equality and justice, not leading the opposition to these values.

Mohler acknowledges that many of the teachings in the Bible are out of step with what we know from reason and experience. Indeed, the data are conclusive and unassailable. When women are well educated, politically and economically engaged, and reproductively self-determined, everyone is better off. Families are more prosperous, societies are more stable, economies are more prosperous, and political systems are more peaceful. If experience counts as evidence, then we need to dismiss the biblical view of women as outmoded and outdated—and a scourge on humanity.

Let me cite one more empirical argument against the Bible as the authoritative revelation from the one true God. It concerns human suffering. How can an all-knowing, all-powerful, and all-good God allow such ungodly havoc to rain down upon so many innocent people in the world? Even if you argue that no one ends up living a blameless life, which no one does, why should infants and children suffer as much as they do?

I could enumerate countless natural disasters where children were swept away by the ravaging sea or crushed to death by falling boulders. I could tell myriad stories of young boys who were brutalized by their fathers and young girls who were kidnapped into sex slavery. And here's one I take personally: my niece Krista, a delightfully playful child, was diagnosed with a brain tumor at age three and, eight years and five surgeries later, died at age eleven. What did Krista do to deserve such a fate? If God can heal the sick and raise the dead, then why did God choose not to restore Krista to health?

Some devout believers respond that God has a plan, which is beyond our knowledge or understanding. As the prophet Isaiah reports (55:8): "For my thoughts are not your thoughts, nor are your ways my ways, says the Lord." Did Krista's painful suffering and tragic death serve some greater cosmic good or moral purpose? If so, her loss certainly contradicts all the evidence I can see of what's good or moral.

Or perhaps God wanted Krista in heaven. Given what the Bible says about heaven, the place is already perfect—and certainly perfect enough that any shortfall isn't worth eight years of suffering by an innocent child. Or maybe God needed someone to sing alto in the angel choir. If so, what happened to the previous alto? Did she miss too many notes and get sent to reform heaven—or wherever wayward angels go? (According to some accounts, wayward angels get sent back to Earth, which would be fine, or to hell, which wouldn't.)

Even if the pain and suffering on Earth serve some divine purpose or cosmic good, it's not a purpose or good that I wish to serve during my brief stay on this planet. An all-knowing God would know better. An all-powerful God would act better. Contrary to the testimony of the Bible, the evidence abounds that God is neither all-knowing nor all-powerful.

Sometimes I wish I were wrong. The idea of a God who ensures that everything will ultimately be all right is enormously appealing. The Bible says (Romans 8:28) that "all things work together for good for those who love God"—a lovely sentiment. It just happens to be wrong. Sometimes things work out for ill, and sometimes things don't work out at all. Without an authoritative revelation from a supernatural God, life can sometimes be lonely, even bewildering.

Matthew Arnold expresses this poignant wistfulness in his poem "Dover Beach," which ranks as one of the most famous and best-loved poems in the English language. Written in the mid-nineteenth century, the poem acknowledges the sadness that inevitably comes when human beings discover that the tide of belief in a supernatural God has gone out. The land of dreams about such a God, it turns out, was always a mirage.

Standing at a window overlooking the sea, watching the moonlight play upon the coast and the sea spray lash the shoreline, the poet says:

*Listen! You hear the grating roar*
*Of pebbles which the waves draw back, and fling,*
*At their return, up the high strand,*
*Begin, and cease, and then again begin,*
*With tremulous cadence slow, and bring*
*The eternal note of sadness in.*

Why the sadness? Arnold continues:

*The Sea of Faith*
*Was once, too, at the full, and round earth's shore*
*Lay like the folds of a bright girdle furl'd.*
*But now I only hear*
*Its melancholy, long, withdrawing roar,*
*Retreating, to the breath*
*Of the night-wind, down the vast edges drear*
*And naked shingles of the world.*

In the wake of faith's retreat, Arnold says, we are left to our own devices. Things we once thought God had created independent of us— joy, light, certitude, peace—turn out to be up to us. Arnold writes:

*Ah, love, let us be true*
*To one another! For the world, which seems*
*To lie before us like a land of dreams,*
*So various, so beautiful, so new,*
*Hath really neither joy, nor love, nor light,*
*Nor certitude, nor peace, nor help for pain;*

Of the six elements of human experience that Arnold mentions in these lines, the key element is certitude. The modern era begins when we realize that certainty is based not on divine revelation apart from us, but rather on human experience among us—hence Arnold's admonition: "let us be true to one another."

This discovery that the tide of supernatural faith has withdrawn can be confusing, as Arnold notes in the final lines of the poem:

*And we are here as on a darkling plain*
*Swept with confused alarms of struggle and flight,*
*Where ignorant armies clash by night.*

The clash between a world decreed by divine revelation and a world illuminated by human reason and experience roiled Arnold's world, and it continues to roil ours as well. It's a battle over what evidence we use to make decisions about what to believe and how to live.

For me, at least, that battle is over. I've staked my claim on life in the modern world, a world not created by divine command or sustained by divine plan. We now turn to the question of how the modern world is put together and what sustains it.

## CHAPTER 3

# What There Is

## *The Nature of Existence*

One summer morning during a week's vacation at the beach, my then-four-year-old daughter Zoë and I were wading along the shoreline at low tide. We were picking up bits of aquatic flora and fauna to put in her sand bucket. Soon we had collected a cast of hermit crabs, a few snails, lots of seaweed, and even a pipefish or two.

As we puttered about in the water, a boat motored quietly up and anchored nearby. The man in it slipped overboard with a clam rake and started the laborious job of raking the sea bottom. Each time he brought the rake to the surface, he picked the clams out of the seaweed and threw them into a laundry basket floating inside an old inner tube. The seaweed went back into the water.

After watching from a distance, Zoë and I decided to have a closer look. We waded out toward the boat, a weary-looking wooden affair that had once been bright blue but now was merely bluish. The name of the man in the water, himself weatherworn and weary-looking as well, turned out to be Short Dog. "My friends call me Shorty for short," he added.

He asked where we were from, and when told Manhattan, he exclaimed, "Manhattan! God bless you for living in a place like that! Myself, I've lived in that town just across the bay there all my life— except for the time I spent in Vietnam." He paused as though he had more to say on the topic, but then he changed his mind and didn't.

After he asked what I did for a living, he explained that he worked as a handyman at a local motel during the week and then went fishing and clamming on the weekends. "I have orders for ten dozen clams for a wedding party tonight and another eight dozen for a restaurant," he said.

When I asked if he would have any extra clams for sale (Zoë could polish off a dozen or two on her own), he said I should check back with him in several hours, but the answer would probably be yes. "If the clamming is good," he added. He then lowered his rake and went back to work.

Midafternoon, I waded back out to where Shorty was still digging away. This time, I went alone. "I'm glad you came back," he called out as I approached. "I'm about to head home, but I have lots of extra clams. Take whatever you want."

Before I put his clams in Zoë's now-empty sand bucket, I asked about the going price. "Just take them," he insisted with a dismissive wave of his hand.

I persisted, however, and he finally told me that he charged his customers three dollars a dozen. "Can you spare three dozen?" I asked.

"Do what you gotta do," he responded. "It don't matter to me."

I took three dozen clams from his floating basket and put ten dollars in the basket with the remaining clams, as he instructed. I thanked him and turned to wade to shore, when he started talking again.

"Your daughter is very beautiful," he said. "Seeing her playing there on the beach reminds me of my time in Vietnam. You know, we would go into villages and simply level them. Everybody died. Everybody."

He paused with a far-off look on his face, while I waited there with him, the sun shining down on us, the waves lapping gently at our waists.

Then he spoke again, softly this time.

"The one nightmare I still have, even after all these years, is of a little girl about your daughter's age. My company—there were about thirty of us—walked into a village one day and she came running out. She wasn't more than ten feet away, reaching her arms out toward us, when suddenly she disappeared. She just disappeared. Someone had strapped a grenade around her waist and sent her out."

His voice trailed off into the sound of the waves.

He told me more: about getting caught one night in a firefight along Rocket Alley, about only three of his company surviving by fleeing into the woods, about his one buddy subsequently dying of his wounds and the other committing suicide a year after he returned home. He also talked about his nightmares and the time he spent in a mental hospital, about losing his marriage, about finding a job and trying to put his life back together again.

And he talked about his son. "He was the one good thing in my life," he said. "I always thought I did pretty well by him: raised him right and everything. And then one night about midnight a cop showed up at my door and said my son had been shot dead in a fight outside a bar here in town."

"When I heard the news, I grabbed my gun and headed for the door. But a neighbor of mine stopped me on the porch. 'That's not the answer, Shorty,' he said. My neighbor was right, of course. But it was hard to take that after everything else."

He paused again, and we watched a sailboat work its way through the waves.

"That's mostly why I come out clamming whenever I can," he said. "I like the feel of being in the water with the sun on my back. I feel comfortable here. It almost seems like I'm going to be all right, like someday I will be able to watch a little girl play and not have nightmares."

I saw Shorty a number of times over the following few seasons, but I haven't seen him since. I don't know if he's all right today or not. I hope so, but one never knows.

My vocation as a pastor—the word "vocation" means "calling"— requires me to have something to say when people come to me whose lives have been devastated by tragedy. Harrowing losses, failed relationships, wayward children, grim diagnoses: people who suffer ill fortune rightly wonder what's going on. Why did this happen? What did I do to deserve it? Am I going to be all right?

If I believed in an all-powerful, all-knowing supernatural God, I'd have ready-made answers to deploy. The scriptures say that God has everything under control and that we shouldn't worry ourselves when bad things happen because, one way or another, either in this life or the next, good people will eventually be all right. As I concluded in the previous chapter, however, not only is there no logical reason to believe such a God exists, there's ample empirical evidence that such a God doesn't.

Since I don't believe in a supernatural God, I need a different response. One could look at the evidence presented by life and conclude that life is absurd, a view championed most notably by German novelist Franz Kafka and French philosopher Albert Camus. Our common use of the word "absurd" resonates with overtones of its ancient origins, which suggest that something is out of tune or discordant; applied to life, "absurd" comes to mean incongruous, even senseless.

To illustrate his point, Camus invokes the ancient Greek myth of Sisyphus, an exceptionally wily king of Corinth who, when Hades arrived to take him to the Underworld, handcuffed Hades and imprisoned him in a trunk. To punish Sisyphus for this treachery, the gods sentenced him to roll a boulder up a mountain. Each time Sisyphus approached the summit, however, the boulder would slip from his control and roll back to the bottom of the mountain. Whereupon Sisyphus would put his shoulder to the boulder and push it back up. In the story, this cycle of senseless labor repeats itself forever.

That's life, according to Camus: an endless struggle without apparent meaning or purpose. Camus contemplates escape from this desperate circumstance, either by suicide or by a "leap of faith" into believing in the idea of God. In the end, Camus rejects both forms of escape and counsels revolt—a willingness to reject the possibility of meaning. Of course, such counsel in the face of absurdity could only be, if in truth life is absurd, itself absurd. Nonetheless, in a state of existential freedom, no ethical rules apply. The only integrity individuals can hope to achieve comes by following their own passion in a world where everything is permitted. Camus accepts this verdict on life not as "an outburst of relief or of joy, but rather a bitter acknowledgment of a fact" ("The Myth of Sisyphus," p. 67).

Especially on days when the tragedies and travesties of life come rolling down like an avalanche, I admit that Camus has a point. Life usually gives us sufficient evidence to convict it of whatever we charge it with. Open the newspaper on even the slowest news day, and you'll see enough caprice and chaos to make you agree with Camus. In one of the most famous laments ever written, Shakespeare's Macbeth declared that "Life...is a tale told by an idiot, full of sound and fury, signifying nothing" (2.1.24–28).

While an occasionally tempting response, the absurdity explanation ultimately fails, especially at the margins where life is best and worst. In fact, we know why bad things happen: they happen either because of nature's indifference or because of human wickedness. The natural world remains profoundly indifferent to our preference for human life over other forms of existence, which is why when lightning strikes or the earth quakes or tumors grow, people suffer. And sometimes people choose, either because they lack sympathy or because they bear malice, to act in ways that cause others to suffer. Bad experiences are anything but absurd.

Nor does absurdity account for the persistence in the world of so much beauty, goodness, and happiness. Anyone who bothers to look can see that the universe as we experience it isn't ultimately chaotic. Beauty depends on well-ordered physical relationships, goodness requires well-ordered ethical relationships, happiness derives from well-ordered emotional relationships—none of which are possible if life is senseless and meaningless.

The question is this: if life isn't absurd and hasn't been designed according to the will of a supernatural God, then what's going on? What makes beauty, goodness, and happiness possible and tragedy and wickedness identifiable?

Physicists tell us that the universe began 15 billion years ago in a moment of utter simplicity. Everything that now exists was compressed into a super-dense particle of energy smaller than a golf ball. As the word itself suggests, the universe was simple, unified, one. When the founding particle began to differentiate itself into various elements and substances, it did so in a way that enabled the universe to become a cosmos: an orderly, coherent whole.

From the beginning of human history, our predecessors wondered how this happened and what it means. In all likelihood, they didn't begin by speculating about everything all at once; they wondered about something in particular: the arc of the moon through the night sky, for example, or the ebb and flow of the sea tides. Eventually, someone wondered whether these events might be related and discovered that the answer is yes. Curiosity about anything ultimately expands into an attempt to explain everything.

Alfred North Whitehead called the effort to explain everything "speculative philosophy." One of the leading thinkers of the twentieth century, Whitehead began his career in mathematics and logic. He and Bertrand Russell collaborated in the writing of *Principia Mathematica* between 1910 and 1913. Whitehead then turned his focus to other modes of explanation, publishing *Religion in the Making* in 1926 (when he was sixty-five), followed three years later by *Process and Reality*, the landmark volume that gave the name to an approach to philosophy that became Whitehead's hallmark: process philosophy.

Whitehead's goal in his philosophical endeavor was "to frame a coherent, logical, necessary system of general ideas in terms of which every element of our experience can be interpreted" (*Process and Reality*,

p. 3). He was looking for a way to think about our experience of the world that would be comprehensive (it would include "every element" of our experience), coherent (the parts would all fit together), logical (nothing supernatural or magical), and—perhaps most important— necessary (careful examination of our experience of the world inevitably leads to these ideas).

In order to map these general ideas, we need to chart the world of our experience: we need to read the book of nature. Admittedly, it's a very big book, and the question of what exactly it contains has always been a puzzle. Theologians call this question the ontological question—the question of being.

In one of my philosophy courses in college, I came across a quote by the twentieth-century American philosopher W. V. Quine from his 1948 essay titled, "On What There Is." I typed it up and stuck it onto the wall in front of my desk. Several decades later, I still have my original copy of the quote. The print has faded, but the quote still tantalizes me. And it's still on my desk. Quine begins his essay with this explanation:

> A curious thing about the ontological problem is its simplicity. It can be put in three Anglo-Saxon monosyllables: "What is there?" It can be answered, moreover, in a word—"Everything"—and everyone will accept this answer as true. However, this is merely to say that there is what there is. There remains room for disagreement over cases; and so the issue has stayed alive down the centuries. (p. 1)

What is there? Everything. And we don't even know the half of it. In fact, the physical entities that we know about constitute less than 1 percent of the universe as a whole. And what we can see makes up a slim fraction of what we know about.

Even so, what we can see is a lot, and nowhere is this more apparent than in the night sky. On a clear night under a dark sky, you can easily see the broad swath of shimmering light our human ancestors rightly called the Milky Way, the relatively commonplace galaxy of which our solar system is an undistinguished part. In addition to the star we call the Sun, our Milky Way galaxy is home to somewhere between 100 million and 400 million additional stars and probably again as many planets.

Two favorite sights in the night sky captivate my attention. I remember vividly the first time I trained my first telescope—a 6″ Dobsonian reflector—on the exquisite planet Saturn, to my eye the most magical of all celestial sights. Especially when its rings are tilted earthward, Saturn will take your breath away. As the science writer Timothy Ferris says in his book *Seeing in the Dark*, "Some call Saturn too good to be true, whatever that may mean" (p. 196).

My other favorite sight is the Andromeda Galaxy, which appears in a small telescope as a faint but unmistakable smudge of light. Made up of something like a trillion stars, the Andromeda Galaxy is the most distant object that can be seen with the unaided eye. Of the more than 125 billion galaxies strewn across our universe, Andromeda is our closest neighbor. The light now reaching Earth from Andromeda began its light-speed journey toward us more than 2 million years ago.

On my office wall at All Souls hangs a stunning photograph of the Andromeda Galaxy, which the talented astrophotographer Robert Gendler compiled by combining more than forty hours of exposures. Whenever I glance up from my desk and see Andromeda, it reminds me that what's closest at hand remains impossibly far away, and what we see most clearly remains mostly indistinct. We don't yet know enough about the book of nature to know what we don't know.

For this reason, as Quine noted, people through the centuries have disagreed about what there is. The basic tussle has pitted people who believe the world is fundamentally material against those who believe it is fundamentally spiritual. Each side has also faced a daunting challenge: accounting for the aspect of experience they don't believe is fundamental. If the world is fundamentally spiritual, where does matter come from? If the world is fundamentally material, where do ideas and consciousness come from?

Ralph Waldo Emerson begins his lecture "The Transcendentalist" with the following observation:

> As thinkers, mankind have ever divided into two sects, Materialists and Idealists; the first class founding on experience, the second on consciousness; the first class beginning to think from the data of the senses, the second class perceive that the senses are not final, and say, the senses give us representations of things, but what are the things themselves, they cannot tell. The materialist insists on facts, on history, on the force of circumstances and the animal wants of man; the idealist on the power of Thought and of Will, on inspiration, on miracle, on individual culture. (p. 193)

Plato and most Christian thinkers have led the charge for the idealists over the centuries. They insist that the basic nature of things is spiritual and that the important and lasting part of a human being is the soul, whatever that may be. Matter, in this view, is only a temporary creation of a divine, cosmic mind. The Christian New Testament says that "God is spirit, and those who worship him must worship in spirit and in truth" (John 4:24). If you believe God is spirit, then it's easy to see why only spirit truly matters.

Two centuries before Plato, however, a school of philosophers from Miletus in Asia Minor began charting an alternative approach. They rejected the view that the gods were somehow responsible for the world as we experience it. Initially, they looked at the four elements they thought made up the world—earth, air, fire, and water—and wondered which one came first. Thales, the founder of the Milesian school, thought fire was the originative substance. Recognizing the difficulty of explaining how fire could become everything else, his students looked for an underlying substance or principle that would account for all four.

While these initial answers turned out to be wrong, the Milesian approach changed how people tried to explain their world. In so doing, they initiated the discipline we now call science. Bolstered by Aristotle and sustained by centuries of observation and research, materialists today—most scientists among them—attempt to explain mind, consciousness, and spirit as interaction among substances.

Ludwig Wittgenstein, a passionate materialist in his early writings, insisted that philosophy could proceed only by pointing to material facts. In his *Tractatus Logico-Philosophicus*, Wittgenstein says, "The right method of philosophy would be this: To say nothing except what can be said, *i.e.* the propositions of natural science" (6.53). When it came to more fundamental explanations, which Wittgenstein referred to derisively as saying "something metaphysical," he was adamant: "Whereof one cannot speak, thereof one must be silent" (7).

I refuse to take Wittgenstein's counsel. The facts of the material world pose puzzles that the material world alone can't answer. Take the person we call Galen Guengerich, for example. I am an organism made up of about 195 pounds of organic material that constitutes roughly 50 trillion individual cells. These cells are differentiated into various tissues and organs, which together make up the ten major systems in the human body. I am 60 percent hydrogen hydroxide, also known as water. And so on. Is this an adequate explanation of who I am? Not even close.

On the other hand, disregarding the physical substrate of the person we call Galen Guengerich doesn't seem right either. The particulars of my body are a non-trivial part of who I am: white, male, straight, prone to certain genetically inherited defects of the eye and thyroid, as well as certain culturally inherited tendencies to eat too much pie. Take all that away, and Galen Guengerich somehow isn't Galen Guengerich anymore.

So what's the answer? It lies in Shorty's boat—as it once might have been described by the Oracle at the ancient Greek Temple of Delphi. As described by Antoine Danchin in *The Delphic Boat: What Genomes Tell Us*, the Oracle of Delphi provided the Greeks with their most authoritative and revered source of knowledge. When asked to answer questions or predict the future, the Pythia, as the priestess who served as the Oracle was known, often responded with riddle-like answers. Croesus, reputed to be the richest man in the world, once asked her if he should invade Persia. She replied, "If you do, a great kingdom will fall." Croesus invaded, and a great kingdom did fall: his own.

The most famous of the Oracle's pronouncements concerned a boat made of planks. What is it that makes the boat a boat? As time passes, some of the planks rot and must be replaced. There eventually comes a time when none of the original planks are left. The boat looks the same, but in material terms, it has changed completely. Is it still the same boat?

Shorty would say yes, this is my boat. Even if none of the materials from which it was originally built remain, this is still my boat. Even if the original planks were pine and the replacement planks are oak, so that a boat once made of pine is now a boat made of oak, this is still my boat. What is important about the planks, according to the Oracle, is not what they are made of, but that they are shaped so that they relate to each other in a certain way. In other words, Shorty's boat is not the material it is made from, but something much more interesting: the boat is the relationship among the planks and the relationship between the collection of planks that constitutes the boat and the people (Shorty) and the world (Gardiner's Bay) around it.

The celebrated American poet Walt Whitman applies this principle to everything. Whitman's "Song of Myself," perhaps his best-known poem, opens with these lines:

*I celebrate myself, and sing myself,*
*And what I assume you shall assume,*
*For every atom belonging to me as good belongs to you.*

*My tongue, every atom of my blood, form'd from this soil, this air,*
*Born here of parents born here from parents the same, and their parents*
    *the same,*
*I, now thirty-seven years old in perfect health begin,*
*Hoping to cease not till death. (1–3, 6–9)*

Whitman begins this song of himself with a tale of atoms and ancestry. He says that he is made of atoms, which were thought in his day to be the most fundamental units of matter. Certain atoms had been drawn from the soil and the air by previous generations of human beings, who had structured them in a distinctive way to yield up the self of whom Whitman now sings. Those atoms are part of the story, but they are not the whole story.

In "Song of Myself," Whitman refers to himself by name only once: "Walt Whitman, a kosmos" (line 497). The opposite of chaos, a cosmos is an orderly, harmonious self-inclusive system. The term "cosmos" often refers to the entire universe as an orderly, harmonious whole.

This reference to himself as a cosmos explains Whitman's statement that "every atom belonging to me as good belongs to you." Whitman's central insight is that the self exists in a system where everyone is who they are by virtue of their relationships to everyone and everything else. Whitman writes:

*And these tend inward to me, and I tend outward to them,*
*And such as it is to be of these more or less I am,*
*And of these one and all I weave the song of myself. (327–329)*

*I know I am solid and sound,*
*To me the converging objects of the universe perpetually*
*  flow . . . (403–404)*

The essence of an individual, according to Whitman, is made up of all the relationships he or she represents. If teased all the way out in space and all the way back in time, these relationships ultimately include everything whatsoever. Some of these relationships appear trivial—unless we consider that everything had to happen precisely as it did for us to be here today, just as we are. It turns out that the story of Galen Guengerich, the cosmos, began not on September 3, 1957, or even nine months earlier than that, but in the beginning.

On these terms, I am best described as the collection of relationships I represent. I was born on a dairy farm in a Mennonite community in central Delaware, grew up in the late 1960s and early 1970s in south Arkansas, and attended a Mennonite high school in Lancaster, Pennsylvania. My father is a Mennonite minister. My niece Krista died of a brain tumor at age eleven. I studied classics at Franklin & Marshall College, theology at Princeton Seminary, and religion and ethics at the University of Chicago. I married young as a Mennonite, divorced when I left the church, and then married again and had a daughter, Zoë, whose mother and I later divorced. Zoë was dedicated in the chancel at All Souls, where I am the minister, and my wife Holly and I were married there as well.

These experiences, and countless others besides, make me who I am—not in the way a potter applies steady pressure to shape a bowl, but in the way flour, butter, sugar, and other ingredients go together to make a cake. If you take away the relational ingredients that make up my life, what remains has little value—certainly not as Galen Guengerich. I'm not a collection of atoms alone, but a collection of experiences that involve both my dedicated atoms and everything else.

This is the founding principle of all existence: everything is constituted by relationships. If you could disassemble the material universe into its constituent elementary particles (there are currently twelve: six quarks and six leptons) and pack them tight together, you'd have a mere handful of material. (Granted, it would be quite a handful!) Everything else is relationships: the experience over time of these particles as they relate to each other.

The key aspect of this picture for us is the experience over time of the particles—what Whitman called the inward and outward flow of atoms. Heraclitus, an ancient Greek philosopher who predated both Plato and Aristotle, famously described the universe as being continually in motion, flowing from one moment to the next. As reported by Plato, Heraclitus says that all things move and nothing remains still, and he likens the universe to the current of a river, saying that you cannot step twice into the same stream. (*Cratylus*, 402a).

Rejecting (for the most part) the basic idealism of Plato and the basic materialism of Aristotle, Alfred North Whitehead developed Heraclitus's insight into a speculative philosophy—a system of general ideas we can use to interpret our experience. Instead of speaking of the world in term of particles, however, Whitehead speaks of a world made up of sequences of energy-events, each of which is constituted by its relationships. The interesting thing for Whitehead was how the universe flows from one moment of experience to the next.

At a given instant, the many experiences that constitute the universe become one tableau: the river caught in a snapshot, with the leaf by the sharp rock and the frog on the bank. But somehow, in the next instant, the many that have become one become a different many becoming one: the leaf just downstream of the sharp rock and the frog in mid-leap. In Whitehead's words, "The many become one, and are increased by one" (*Process and Reality*, p. 21).

As the universe accumulates experiences in this way, Whitehead then wondered, how do future experiences get decided? And where do past experiences go? In future chapters, we will explore these questions more fully. The answers will help us understand how we as human beings can live each moment of experience most fully and enable the future to develop most beneficially.

In the meantime, Whitehead's claim that we are constituted by our relationships has one sobering consequence. We often view ourselves as independent creatures, able to make our own way in the world and choose our own course. If Whitehead is correct, and I believe he is, then the opposite is true. As Whitehead once put it, "...we are factors in the universe, and are dependent on the universe for every detail of our experience" (*Essays in Science and Philosophy*, p. 78).

This principle applies to everything whatsoever. Nothing—not atoms, not people, not galaxies—is what it is strictly within itself. Everything that exists is made up of constituent parts that are borrowed from, shared with, and related to others outside it. As humans, we are utterly dependent upon the parents who conceived us, the plants and animals that daily give their lives for our nourishment, the trees that reverse our cycle of taking in oxygen and giving off carbon dioxide, and the sun that warms the atmosphere and lights our path. In every respect, we are utterly dependent.

This principle does not mean that our future is wholly determined by outside forces, however. Within the constraints imposed by the relationships that constitute us, we have options for how to move forward. Think of it this way: the past is the raw material out of which we construct the future. You and I each have before us a unique collection of materials—the circumstances of our birth, our talents, our past relationships, the skills we have developed, and the mistakes we have made. Within the limits imposed by those materials, we are free to build the future in whatever way we choose. We live at the intersection of prologue and possibility.

Whitehead puts this principle as follows. Each moment of life, he says, "arises as an effect facing its past and ends as a cause facing its future" (*Adventures of Ideas*, p. 194). The present moment is an effect of the past and a cause of the future. This is how what there is comes into being—the way time moves forward, history unfolds, and human life proceeds. Within the range of options we have available at any given time, we employ the resources made available by the past in order to create the future. The present builds a bridge from what is past to what is possible.

The question before us is how to construct that bridge and whether religion forms a part of it. As I will discuss in upcoming chapters, religious faith and practice at their best can help liberate us from the limitations of the past and help us construct a more promising future. Religion is about transformation—about making good on our desire to become better people and make our world a better place.

For most people throughout most of Western history, however, religion has been an agent not of transformation and liberation, but of the opposite. The world supposedly created by God the Father and supposedly redeemed by God the Son (or, in the case of Judaism and Islam, created by an apparently male God and authoritatively guided by a male prophet) has been oppressively maintained over the centuries by their almost exclusively male minions. The physical and institutional violence wielded by men in service of the patriarchal underpinnings of Western culture has not only destroyed entire populations of unbelievers, it has also relegated certain classes of people—most notably women and gays—to the status of second-class citizens.

My own conviction is that the dominant paradigms of Western culture—a male-dominant approach to religion and an individual-centered approach to everything—must be challenged at their points of greatest strength, not merely at their points of greatest weakness. It's not good enough to argue that Jesus was attentive to women in distress and therefore we should demonstrate a similar paternal charity toward women today. We need to examine this worldview as a whole and ask where it comes from—its epistemological (how we know) and ontological (what there is) foundations. What we have discovered, and will continue to discover, is that the religions of the West developed as they did for reasons that made sense at the time, but their time has passed. Our understanding of how we know and of what there is must evolve, and our understanding of God must evolve as well.

Admittedly, my discussion in this chapter has featured many of the usual suspects: a collection of mostly European and mostly white males, almost all of them dead. Given the identity of these messengers, myself included, it's easy to underestimate how innovative, even revolutionary, this way of thinking will turn out to be. For my part, I'll try my best to keep out in front of me the fact that I'm doing this work as a straight white male of significant cultural privilege. Perhaps ironically, I am trying to change the theological underpinnings of a culture that has served my individual interests rather well, at least as those interests have been traditionally defined. But I am committed to helping religion evolve—not for the purpose of increasing my own suffering, though that may need to happen, but to enable others to flourish.

For this to happen, theology needs to proceed from a different foundation than traditional religion has established. Otherwise, theology and culture become mutually self-reinforcing. As the contemporary theologian Marjorie Suchocki demonstrates in her influential 1983 lecture at Xavier University titled "Weaving the World," theology not only reflects the perspectives of a society, it also reinforces and shapes those perspectives. In the case of women, she says, "When theology supports and encourages the idea of woman as childlike, or as the source of evil, or as possession, or as primarily emotional and not overly given to intelligence, as essentially dependent, then feminists claim that theology is at that point invidious and simply wrong" (p. 77).

Suchocki goes on to say that process thought addresses feminist and liberationist critiques of traditional theology by insisting that existence is based not on our separation from each other by position or power but on our relation to each other. "Relationships intertwine our existence, qualifying each other and intensifying each other according to the creative responses and purposes of each of us," Suchocki says. "On an ontological level, process thought suggests that this experience of human existence as relational is not an exception to all other forms of existence, but is an exemplification of what existence is about" (p. 80).

Suchocki foreshadows the consequences of this approach—consequences we will discuss in upcoming chapters:

> But if all existence is relational, then who and how and what we are likewise has an effect upon all else in the universe—some maximally, and most minimally, but an effect nonetheless. It matters, this becoming of ours, and not only to and for ourselves. We actually make a difference in the whole of this awesome universe (p. 81).... To perceive oneself existing interdependently in the world calls for responsible thought and action toward injustice anywhere in the world. I am affected by it and affect it. (p. 82)

If everything depends on everything else, then everyone bears responsibility, at least in some measure, greater or less, for everyone and everything else. We influence how the past becomes the future. For that, we are responsible.

## CHAPTER 4

# What's Divine

## *The Experience of God*

**W**hen people meet with me in my study, the reason is usually pastoral. After we exchange pleasant greetings and settle into comfortable chairs, the news tumbles out, and it's usually not good. My mother just died yesterday, and my siblings and I can't agree on whether to bury or cremate her. My brother was arrested last week on felony charges. My best friend is having an affair, and I don't know whether to tell her husband, who is also a good friend. My son was just asked to leave his school. I lost my job four months ago, and I'm about to be evicted from my apartment. My doctor tells me I have six months to live.

My role in these situations is to provide comfort. I gently suggest that even though part of your life may indeed be falling apart, not everything has. You still have friends who stand with you and a community of faith that supports you. Together we can find strength to face the present, courage to redeem the past, and imagination to chart the future.

Usually in these conversations, we focus on the matter at hand and how to endure or overcome it. But sometimes people ask the theological question that lurks behind the existential crisis: how could God let this happen? People who believe in God feel abandoned. Even people who don't believe in God feel enraged at the God they don't believe in. The human conviction that the universe is the kind of place where someone should be in charge of outcome runs deep.

We come by this belief naturally. A 2009 *Science* magazine article by Elizabeth Culotta on the origin of religion cites research by Justin Barrett and others at the University of Oxford in England. Barrett observes that humans have an innate tendency to see signs of "agents"—minds like our own—at work in the world. Because we experience cause and effect in our daily lives, we tend to assume that everything in the world ultimately results from the action of an agent. Rather than ascribing events to random causes or mechanistic forces, humans prefer teleological, or purpose-driven, explanations.

The article cites several studies involving young children, who were asked why rocks are pointy. Are they pointy because they are composed of small bits of material or to keep animals from sitting on them? Most answered, "To keep animals from sitting on them." Even children prefer explanations that attribute purpose to inanimate objects. What happens when you write this teleological preference cosmically large? "You begin to see that a god is a likely thing for a human mind to construct," concludes Deborah Kelemen of Boston University (p. 786).

It's true that attributing a given outcome to the action of an intelligent being doesn't mean an intelligent being didn't cause it. But throughout human history, human beings have been remarkably consistent at wrongly attributing events—both cosmic and mundane—to supernatural deities. In her masterful and compelling book titled *A History of God*, historian Karen Armstrong points out that the ancients believed the Sky God ruled the human realm through a series of intermediary deities, the forces of nature: sun, wind, water, fire, thunder, and lightning. In order to appease these often ferocious gods and keep the cosmic order intact, humans adopted the practice of animal sacrifice. Over time, they realized that their sacrifices had no bearing on the caprice of nature's gods. Eventually, they realized that the forces of nature had other causes.

Yet some form of belief in God has persisted over the course of human history. Out of a world population of 6.8 billion in 2011, the three major monotheisms count one-half the population among their adherents: 2.2 billion Christians, 1.5 billion Muslims, and 15 million Jews. Hinduism, with its wide-ranging conceptions of the divine, accounts for another 950 million. Whatever we might say about the

logical or empirical foundation of the beliefs espoused by adherents
to these faiths, we certainly must acknowledge the appeal of belief in
some kind of God. Two-thirds of the population of the Earth is too
large a sample size to dismiss out of hand. Then again, everyone once
believed the Earth stood at the center of the solar system.

As we noted in chapter two, the twentieth-century German philosopher Ludwig Wittgenstein argues, using his language game analogy, that even beliefs that have no logical or empirical foundation can
nonetheless help believers make sense of their lives and their world.
Karen Armstrong makes a similar point from a historical perspective.
Armstrong says that " . . . it is far more important for a particular idea of
God to *work* than for it to be logically or scientifically sound. As soon as
it ceases to be effective it will be changed—sometimes for something
radically different" (p. xxi).

When Armstrong says that it is important for a particular idea of
God to "work," I take her to mean that the idea needs to explain
human experience in a satisfactory way, especially experience of the
divine. It also needs to provide comfort in times of distress and explain
satisfactorily how agency gets allocated and power gets mediated, both
in heaven and on Earth. What counts as satisfying, however, can vary
widely from one generation to the next.

Armstrong intends her book to be not a history of the reality of
God, but a history of the way Jews, Christians, and Muslims have
perceived God over the course of the past several thousand years. The
statement "I believe in God," she observes, has had and continues to
have contradictory and even mutually exclusive meanings. She admits
that fundamentalists in each religion reject this view, since they believe
that the founding prophets all experienced their God in exactly the
same way as people do today.

*Yet if we look at our three religions, it becomes clear that there is no*
*objective view of "God"; each generation has to create the image of*

*God that works for it. The same is true of atheism. "I do not believe
in God" has meant something slightly different at each period of history. . . . Is the "God" who is rejected by the atheists today, the God
of the patriarchs, the God of the prophets, the God of the philosophers,
the God of the mystics or the God of the eighteenth-century deists?
(p. xx)*

In other words, once the impulse to ascribe divine agency had
taken hold, it persisted. It could have faded away. When people discovered that the Sky God didn't control the Wind God, they could
have concluded that God didn't exist. Instead, they ascribed to natural
causes those events they knew to be naturally caused and assigned God
to a different role. The history of God is the history of the roles human
beings needed a god to play in order to bring coherence to human history and human life.

Ironically, the ancient Greek notion that underlies the Christian
doctrine of the Trinity suggests this role-playing function on the part
of the divine. In classical Greek theater, actors wore masks on stage.
Each mask identified a particular character in the play, and the expression depicted by the mask often conveyed an essential trait of the character—a tragic sufferer, for example, or a comic buffoon. These masks
also enabled one actor to play several roles and male actors to play
female characters (only men could serve as actors). They also made it
easier for the audience to keep track of the action.

The ancient Greek word for masks of this kind is *prosopon*,
which translates literally as "face" but can also mean "person." In
Christian doctrine, each person of the Trinity—Father, Son, and
Holy Ghost—is a *prosopon* of God, a face or mask used by a single
divine actor. When wearing the Father mask, according to this view,
God reigns over humanity as creator and judge. God puts on the Son
mask as Jesus, the fully human and fully divine Savior, whose perfect
life and blameless death pays the debt for all human sin. After the

ascension of the risen Christ into heaven, God's presence remains on Earth in the person—the mask—of the Holy Ghost, whose presence guides and comforts. In this way, Christian theology attempts to account for the human experience that, on these terms, God is over us (God the Father), for us (God the Son), and with us (God the Holy Ghost).

For many people over the past two millennia, this image of God has "worked" in the Wittgenstein/Armstrong sense: it has helped make sense of their experience of the world. In so doing, it has also provided deep comfort. But Christian theologians through the centuries have also undertaken to prove that this view of God has firm logical and empirical foundations. These efforts have coalesced into three so-called proofs of the existence of God: the ontological proof, the cosmological proof, and the teleological proof.

The ontological proof received its first formulation from Anselm, the eleventh-century archbishop of Canterbury, who attempted to prove the existence of God using logic alone, without relying on sense experience or other evidence. Anselm defined God as a being "than which nothing greater can be conceived." Because the idea of a greatest possible being exists in the human mind, Anselm argued, it must necessarily exist in reality as well. Why? If the greatest possible being exists only in the mind, then a greater being is possible: one that exists both in the mind and in reality (*Proslogion*, chs. 2 and 3). The ontological argument has received intense scrutiny in the centuries since Anselm. It was criticized by Kant and defended by Hegel, among countless others. More recently, some scholars have suggested that Anselm intended to make a different argument: that existence without the possibility of nonexistence (that is, necessary existence) is greater than existence with the possibility of nonexistence (that is, contingent existence).

The cosmological proof focuses on cause and contingency. Who or what caused the universe? Why is there something rather than nothing?

Even if the universe has eternally existed (a view first advanced by the ancient Greek philosopher Parmenides and later endorsed by both Plato and Aristotle), someone or something had to put it into motion—a "prime mover" or "unmoved mover," in Aristotle's description. If the universe didn't eternally exist, someone or something had to cause it—a "first cause," as Plato suggested. In his influential *Summa Theologica*, Thomas Aquinas, the thirteenth-century theologian who provided an authoritative summary to the cosmological argument, identified the prime mover and first cause: "...to which everyone gives the name 'God'" (I: 2, 3).

For many Christians today, the most convincing proof of the existence of God is the teleological proof—the argument from design, or purpose. Aquinas puts the case as follows: "An orderedness of actions to an end is observed in all bodies obeying natural laws, even when they lack awareness. For their behavior hardly ever varies, and will practically always turn out well; which shows that they truly tend to a goal, and do not merely hit it by accident. Nothing however that lacks awareness tends to a goal, except under the direction of someone with awareness and with understanding; the arrow, for example, requires an archer. Everything in nature, therefore, is directed to its goal by someone with intelligence, and this we call 'God'" (I: 2, 3).

Present-day creationism descends directly from Aquinas, arguing that the wonder and splendor of creation makes the idea of an intelligent designer necessary. One of the more flamboyant versions of this proposal came from astrophysicist Fred Hoyle, whom Richard Dawkins quotes in his book *The God Delusion*. Hoyle, who was making the point that intelligent life almost certainly appeared elsewhere in the universe before it spread to Earth, reportedly said that "the probability of life originating on Earth is no greater than the chance that a hurricane, sweeping through a scrapyard, would have the luck to assemble a Boeing 747" (pp. 137–138). Dawkins counters this claim with an incisive application of the infinite regress argument made by David Hume in the eighteenth century: if complex life requires an intelligent designer, then God must have been designed by a super-intelligent designer, and so on.

Of course, the argument that God must exist in order to fill the gaps in human ignorance has always been a tempting option. Because we don't know what happened before the beginning, if indeed there was a beginning, it's tempting to posit God as the agent of last (or first) resort—and impossible to prove that God doesn't play that role. Nonetheless, if we bother to consider the evidence, the conclusion seems unwarranted. Recent discoveries at the forefront of particle physics suggest that the universe is much more complex than any version of "in the beginning" would suggest. Time and space may be only two of up to eleven dimensions, and our universe may be one of many parallel universes. In addition, our present universe may be one in a countless series of such universes constituted by the set of elementary particles that make it up.

Is it possible to attribute the universe to the creative work of a supernatural God? Yes. Is it necessary? No—and neither is it sensible. A God who could create a universe out of nothing would be hard to believe in. Isaac Newton, in a passage from his *Principia*, begins with the argument from design and then proceeds to enumerate all the qualities the designer must necessarily possess.

> *The most beautiful system of the sun, planets and comets could only proceed from the counsel and dominion of an intelligent and powerful Being. . . . He is eternal and infinite, omnipotent and omniscient; that is, his duration reaches from eternity to eternity; his presence from infinity to infinity; he governs all things and knows all things that are or can be done. (quoted by Armstrong, p. 304)*

If you make the leap of faith required to believe that an intelligent designer is necessary to fill in the gaps in our knowledge, then you have to accept that this designer possesses all the other qualities of a supernatural monotheistic God, such as omniscience and omnipotence. As we discussed in chapter two, the idea of such a God has no logical or empirical foundation. The belief in a God who can and does modify the laws of nature willy-nilly makes no logical sense, as if God could, in response to fervent prayer, change the direction of a fierce storm or empty a parking space near the door of the mall when it's raining. By the same token, the belief in a God who could rescue innocent sufferers but chooses to stand idly by makes no moral sense. If God is able to save innocent sufferers from starving to death or dying young, why does God routinely choose not to do so? As I explained in chapter two, my own conclusion is that God isn't the kind of being who can save innocent sufferers, otherwise God would.

Of course, we have a deep-seated habit of thinking about God's agency—either the God we believe in or the God we don't—as having the same general form as human agency. Take the most powerful human agent you can imagine (and your imagination will doubtless trend toward male agents) and multiply his power by a billion, or by a gazillion, or even by infinity. You still end up with an established power in heaven that looks a lot like the established powers on Earth, which are and have always been mostly male.

One day a woman in my congregation contacted me in a state of advanced apoplexy because she had overheard her two-year-old son talking with his friend about God, and her son referred to God as "he." She told me that she had been determined that her son wouldn't succumb to such silliness. She had read him stories about the ancient belief in goddesses and how the universe came into being with a Big Bang. She had brought him to All Souls, where we don't use gender-specific language for God. She even made sure that his toys and games had more women in positions of power than men.

Even so, after less than thirty months, her son had already drunk the Kool-Aid: God was a male. After commending her on her intention and efforts, I told her that this problem exasperates me too. Male dominance remains so pervasive in our culture that it rarely needs to be asserted. It's the rule to which the occasional female who becomes well known for something other than a fetching face or fulsome figure proves the welcome exception. Yes, we need to change our children's storybooks and toys, but we also need to change the underlying cultural assumptions about how we know and what's divine.

If you accept the conclusion that God isn't supernatural, as I do, then you have to ask whether a conception of God remains at all necessary in our attempt to interpret every aspect of our experience. A central premise of this book, and perhaps its most controversial and counterintuitive claim, is that God is not supernatural, and yet belief in God is necessary. Both atheists and traditional religionists agree about the nature of God; they disagree only about whether this God does or does not exist. For my part, I agree with the atheists that God is not supernatural, yet I agree with the advocates of traditional religion that belief in God is necessary.

My goal is to articulate an understanding of God that enables us to interpret our experience of the world and to account for its meaning without requiring us to make claims about God that contravene the laws of nature. What do we experience as human beings in the modern world that we need a conception of God to make sense of?

This question lies within the domain of theology. Literally translated from the Greek, theology is speech about God. More generally, theology is the process of using language to describe certain kinds of experiences. In its simplest form, theology steps back from religious experience and asks how such experience is possible. It also asks why the experience is transformative or why it is destructive.

For most Americans today, religious experience includes an experience of God—or at least a belief in God. In a recent survey conducted by the Gallup organization, 94 percent of Americans said they believe in God or a supreme being of some kind. Nearly two-thirds believe God is the kind of being with whom one can have a personal relationship.

They could be mistaken, of course. Ludwig Feuerbach was a nineteenth-century German philosopher who attempted to discredit Christianity by disproving the existence of God. His thesis was simple. God is not a divine reality, he argued, but a human creation. Men and women take the ideals for which they long—the control of one's own destiny, the power to act decisively, the knowledge to decide wisely—and project those desires into the realm of the infinite, then worship them. God, he concluded, is nothing more than the mythic fulfillment of a human wish that there were such a being: "Religion is the dream of the human mind" (p. xix).

On one level, Feuerbach's argument is easy to refute. It's true that wishing cannot create something that does not exist, but neither can it obliterate something that does. If I am restless in the night, for example, and wish fervently that the morning would come, that wish does not mean the morning will never come. The fact that people long to have a personal relationship with a supernatural God doesn't mean such a God exists, but neither does the recognition that God isn't supernatural eliminate the desire to experience God. This human longing has been persistent and pervasive throughout human history.

Perhaps the human effort to prove the existence of God with logic and to buttress the belief in God with evidence has been misplaced. Alfred North Whitehead describes an error he calls the fallacy of misplaced concreteness. Where do you look in order to find the most real stuff in the world, the most concrete part of existence? Many people, Plato among them, say that thoughts and ideas are the most concrete things in the world, the most real of the real stuff.

Whitehead argues that this is a fallacy, that the concreteness is misplaced. He suggests that thoughts and ideas are abstractions that emerge from the real stuff of life, which is experience (*Science and the Modern World*, p. 52).

If you want to get in touch with what really matters, talk about experience, not ideas. You can debate ideas until the cows come home; you can disprove them or refute them or define them out of existence. That is because ideas are abstracted from—taken out of— the real stuff of life, which is experience. Our experiences are simply there, being what they are, making claims on our time and attention, making demands on our lives. To return to the question at hand, what do we experience as human beings in the modern world that we need a conception of God to make sense of?

In his groundbreaking 1821 book *The Christian Faith*, Friedrich Schleiermacher proclaimed that the essence of Christian piety is the feeling of absolute dependence upon God. This statement was groundbreaking for two reasons. For the first time, it declared that the essence of religion was not obedience to a set of divine commandments, or assent to orthodox doctrine, or recognition of Jesus as Messiah. Religion is an experience—a feeling, Schleiermacher called it. The liberal tradition in theology flows from this declaration that religion is first and foremost an experience.

What kind of experience does Schleiermacher have in mind? He calls it a feeling of absolute, or unqualified, dependence upon God (pp. 16–18). It's a feeling—an experience—of being connected to everything that exists in a way that both validates our place in the universe and yet reminds us that we are small and temporary creatures.

When newcomers to All Souls tell me that they are spiritual but not religious, which they often do, I ask them what they mean by spiritual. Their response often involves the beach, or the mountains, or the night sky: a place where they have an experience of the sublime—a feeling that unites an experience of the universe's majesty with the experience of our human fragility. In his book *On Religion: Speeches to Its Cultured Despisers*, Schleiermacher describes the feeling of absolute dependence this way:

> *It is as fleeting and transparent as the first scent with which the dew gently caresses the waking flowers, as modest and delicate as a maiden's kiss, as holy and fruitful as a nuptial embrace; indeed not like these but it is itself all of these. A manifestation, an event develops quickly and magically into an image of the universe. Even as the beloved and ever-sought-for form fashions itself, my soul flees toward it; I embrace it, not as a shadow, but as the holy essence itself. I lie on the bosom of the infinite world. At this moment I am its soul, for I feel all its powers and its infinite life as my own; at that moment it is my body, for I penetrate its muscles and its limbs as my own, and its innermost nerves move according to my sense and my presentiment as my own. With the slightest trembling the holy embrace is dispersed, and now for the first time the intuition stands before me as a separate form; I survey it, and it mirrors itself in my open soul like the image of the vanishing beloved in the awakened eye of a youth; now for the first time the feeling works its way up from inside and diffuses itself like the blush of shame and desire on his cheek. This moment is the highest flowering of religion. (p. 32)*

The key sentence is this one: "At this moment I am its soul, for I feel all its powers and its infinite life as my own; at that moment it is my body, for I penetrate its muscles and its limbs as my own, and its innermost nerves move according to my sense and my presentiment as my own." Half a century later, Walt Whitman would invoke this same experience of being intimately and extensively connected to the universe with his inflowing and outflowing of atoms, which made Whitman part of everything and everything part of him.

Hildegard of Bingen, the twelfth-century Christian mystic and proto-feminist, captures this experience in one of her visions:

> *I am the fiery life of divine substance, I blaze above the beauty of the fields, I shine in the waters, I burn in sun, moon, and stars. And I awaken all to life with every wind of the air, as with invisible life that sustains everything. . . . Thus I am concealed in things as fiery energy. They are ablaze through me, like the breath that ceaselessly enlivens the human being, or like the wind-tossed flame in a fire. All these things live in their essence, and there is no death in them, for I am life. I also am rationality, who holds the breath of the resonant word by which the whole of creation was created; and I have breathed life into everything, so that nothing by its nature may be mortal, for I am life. (pp. 172–173)*

For reasons that will become apparent in the next chapter, I believe this experience of being extensively connected to the universe and utterly dependent upon it is an absolutely necessary aspect of a fulfilling human life. It also provides a foundation for the experience I'm referring to when I use the word "God." God is the experience of being connected to all that is—all that is present, as well as all that is past and all that is possible.

When people ask me whether I believe God exists, my answer is yes. I believe God exists in a way similar to the way beauty exists, but not in the way a person or an apple exists. An apple is a physical object that can be weighed and measured. Its physical structure and chemical composition can be described in detail. It can be compared to other kinds of apples and contrasted with other types of fruit. The work of science is to describe apples and explain the processes by which they change over time and fall to the ground. You can pick an apple off a tree, cut it into slices, bake it in a pie, and serve it warm with vanilla ice cream.

God, by contrast, is an experience, akin to our experience of beauty. Beauty itself never appears to us, but we find the idea necessary to account for our delight in the symmetry and form of certain objects and experiences: sunsets, symphonies, and sculptures by Degas. While different in many other respects, beauty and God are both qualities of our experience.

In this sense, the description of our experience of God is a theological task. Rather than trying to describe the physical world and explain its workings, as scientists do, theologians try to interpret human experience and account for its meaning. The periodic table of theological elements is laid out in terms of meaning, purpose, and value. None of these elements can be put under a microscope. Instead, we ask what ideas we need to have about the world in order to interpret our experience and account for its meaning to us.

In addition to the experience of being extensively connected to the universe and utterly dependent upon it, we need a conception of God to account for two other kinds of experience: our experience of all that is past and all that is possible. In his book titled *The Fabric of the Cosmos*, Brian Greene says that one of the deepest unresolved mysteries in modern physics is the mystery called the arrow of time. He notes that we take for granted that there is a direction to the way things unfold in time. For example, "A piping hot pizza cools down en route from Domino's, but we never find a pizza arriving hotter than when it was removed from the oven. Cream stirred into coffee forms a uniformly tan liquid, but we never see a cup of light coffee unstir and separate into white cream and black coffee. Eggs fall, cracking and splattering, but we never see splattered eggs and eggshells gather together and coalesce into uncracked eggs" (p. 143). We can remember the collection of events we call the past, but not the collection of events we call the future. These sequences of events only happen in one temporal order. They always move forward, but never in reverse.

In light of the pervasive evidence of time's arrow, one would think some fundamental law of physics would show why things evolve through one sequence but never the reverse. The perplexing thing, Greene notes, is that no one has discovered any such law. In fact, all the known and accepted laws of physics treat both directions in time alike. Anything that can happen in one direction can theoretically happen in the other—except that it doesn't. Pizza doesn't spontaneously heat up, and eggs don't unscramble.

In a remark that fortunately for most of us is more poetry than physics, Albert Einstein comments on the puzzle of time in a letter to the family of Michele Besso, a physicist friend—and for fifty years Einstein's closest friend—who had died. It was of no consequence that Besso had preceded him in death, Einstein wrote. "People like us, who believe in physics, know that the distinction between past, present and future is only a stubbornly persistent illusion" (Dyson, p. 193).

As Einstein observes, our experience strongly suggests that the past and the future have an enduring presence. You remember what you did yesterday, after all, and you anticipate what you might do tomorrow. Even if your memory turns out to be faulty and your hopes unrealistic, you still experience your past and future as integral to your sense of who you are.

Let's think about where experiences go when they're over and where they come from before they happen. When we think of the most enduring elements of existence, we usually think of physical things: rocks, mountains, and so on. On the other hand, we usually think of the elements that make up the realm of meaning—thoughts, feelings, and emotions—as fleeting and ephemeral. Over time, however, the opposite turns out to be true. The atoms that make up a given body or object eventually disband themselves and go on to constitute something else entirely. Even so, the experiences made possible by those atoms remain, at least in our memories. And the experiences continue really to exist, albeit in a different way.

In her lecture "Weaving the World," Marjorie Suchocki speaks of how her love for her mother continued even after her mother's death:

*Recently my mother died. Our relationship had been deep and rich, but now she is absent to me. I always used to think that in the death of someone we love, a part of the self dies, too, because the self called into existence by the other is no longer so called. Like some untended vine, that portion of the self withers, finally to die with the other. But I think now I was wrong, because it is not like that at all. It came as a perplexity to me the first time I tried to say, "I loved my mother," because the past tense of the verb seemed simply wrong: I still love my mother. But she is no longer there in person to evoke that loving, and love is most certainly relational. What does it mean, that the imme-diacy of loving survives death? I do not mean that sentimentally but ontologically. What does it mean when love continues beyond the time of its reciprocity or evocation by the other? (p. 79)*

Among other things, it means we need to account for how the past continues to vivify the present. Recently, a woman whose partner had died after battling cancer for several years came to see me. It was a harrowing loss: they had been together for nearly three decades, and her partner's death had come just weeks before they could have been married in New York.

"I miss her terribly," she said, her eyes filling with tears. "And sometimes I feel like she's still with me—like she's really there in the room with me."

"Not that I actually see her or anything," she quickly added. She paused a moment, then went on, cautiously: "I sometimes talk to her though. It makes me feel better to be able to say things to her, even though I know she can't reply."

Then she asked the question that had brought her to my office: "Do you think it's OK for me to talk to her like that?" I assured her that it was fine, though I did invite her to return if she ever heard her partner reply to her out loud.

Experiences from the past can have real presence in the present. In fact, they must: it's the only way the present ends up happening.

To return to Marjorie Suchocki's ontological question, however, what does it mean to say that experiences from the past continue to exist? What does "exist" mean, in this case? Surely something more than "exist in memory." Let's say that ten thousand years ago, an infant girl was abandoned on a hillside by her parents. Let's say that no one but her parents ever knew about her, hence no one has remembered her since they died. Let's even say—and I realize that this is a stretch scientifically—that none of the atoms that made up her body are still attached to each other. Even so, the experience of the infant girl still matters. Her suffering remains an integral part of the past that eventually came to constitute the present. It's part of the foundation on which the present is built. Everything in the past had to happen as it did for the present to be what it is.

We need some way to acknowledge the enduring presence of all that is past. The experience of an abandoned girl matters, even if no one has thought about her for ten thousand years. Our experience demands a resting place—a refuge—for all that is past.

We have a word for the totality of the physical world; the word is universe. We also need a word for the unification of all the experiences in the universe; that word is God. Alfred North Whitehead calls this the consequent nature of God, suggesting that God is, in part, the consequence of, and thus constituted by, all experiences whatsoever. This conception of God accounts for our sense that experiences matter. They don't matter just to us; they matter, period. Even though no one may remember them or even know about them in the first place, experiences don't vanish into thin air.

We invoke the experience of God to account for our sense that, just as atoms are never lost in physical reactions, so no human

experience—however tragic—is ever suffered alone or eternally forgotten. As Whitehead puts it, everything that happens in the universe—"its sufferings, its sorrows, its triumphs, its immediacies of joy"
(*Process and Reality*, p. 346)—is woven into the harmony of a completed
whole. God is the name we give to our sense of a presence that bears
witness to everything that happens in life. In Whitehead's words, God
is "the binding element in the universe" (*Religion in the Making*, p. 152).
Without God, our experiences have no refuge, no ultimate resting
place.

We also invoke the experience of God in order to account for our
sense of the future. At any given moment, the future can unfold in a
number of possible ways. These possibilities must come from somewhere. Admittedly, you can't put possibilities under a microscope. But
they have to come from somewhere. Simply put, our experience of
God accounts for our sense that the future is possible at all. Whitehead
calls this God's primordial nature, which points to God's role as the
beginning of the future.

The experience of God also accounts for our sense that the future
will unfold in a way that tends toward meaning and not toward chaos.
When the ancient Greeks pondered the future, they often spoke of fate,
which they understood as the tendency of the future to move toward
a particular goal, like the tendency of a plant to grow toward the sun.
The plant can be turned away, of course, but it will always grow back
toward the light.

In a similar way, the experience of God accounts for our sense that
the future can unfold in a purposive and meaningful way, even though
it sometimes doesn't. God is the transcendent source of possibility—
what Whitehead calls "the eternal urge of desire" (*Process and Reality*, p.
344)—beckoning the universe toward a more fulfilling future. In this way,
our faith in this experience of God gives us hope for a better future.

Even (maybe especially) in a scientific age, human beings continue to long for an experience of being part of something larger than

themselves—an experience of transcendence. Scientific explanations do not satisfy this longing: the more we learn about ourselves and our universe, the more trivial our existence appears to be and the more ephemeral our experience.

When I say "I believe in God," I'm saying that I believe in an experience that intimately and extensively connects me to all that is—all that is present, as well as all that is past, and all that is possible. As the safeguard of all that is past, God provides a refuge—no matter how dire my present circumstances. As the source of all that is possible, God provides hope—no matter how bleak my prospects.

For most people who say they don't believe in God, however, the experience of God as immanent witness to our past experiences and transcendent source of our future possibilities isn't the problem. Their problem is the idea that God is a personal being or, to put the issue more precisely, a conscious being. This is the parking-spot-by-the-mall-door problem. Is God, by virtue of being independent of time and history, able willy-nilly to step in and change things—move the Hummer to parking lot C?

In a word, the answer is no. In my view, people who accept scientific inquiry as a valid way of knowing and yet believe God can change the laws of nature are simply—how shall we say this?—confused. The question is whether, if God is neither personal in the move-the-Hummer sense nor conscious in the human-like sense, we can take the experience of God personally.

In one of his poems, the Pulitzer Prize–winning American poet Stephen Dunn tells a story about the summer that he and his wife sent their young daughter to Arts and Crafts Week at the Smithville Methodist Church. Their daughter liked her little friends and the songs they sang. She also liked twisting and folding paper into dolls.

When she came home with the "Jesus Saves" button, however, they knew, as Dunn puts it, "what art was up, what ancient craft." Even so, they reasoned, what's so bad about Jesus? He was a good man, like Lincoln or Thomas Jefferson, and putting faith in good people is the best way to avoid cynicism.

Then their daughter came home singing "Jesus loves me, the Bible tells me so." It was time for them to talk to her. But what to say? Could they say Jesus doesn't love you? Could they tell her the Bible is a great book some people use to make you feel bad? They soon realized that they couldn't teach disbelief to their child; she needed to hear a wonderful story, and they didn't have a story. So they sent her back without a word.

On parents' night, the children sang one song about Noah's ark and another in which they had to jump up and down for Jesus. Dunn continues:

> *I can't ever remember feeling so uncertain*
> *about what's comic, what's serious.*
>
> *Evolution is magical but devoid of heroes.*
> *You can't say to your child*
> *"Evolution loves you." The story stinks*
> *of extinction and nothing*
>
> *exciting happens for centuries. I didn't have*
> *a wonderful story for my child*
> *and she was beaming. All the way home in the car*
> *she sang the songs,*
>
> *occasionally standing up for Jesus.*
> *There was nothing to do*
> *but drive, ride it out, sing along*
> *in silence. (pp. 183–184)*

You can't say evolution loves you, Dunn rightly insists. Nor, I would add, can you say gravity believes in you or the second law of thermodynamics will transform your life. These ideas are abstract, not personal enough to establish an emotional connection.

In this sense, the idea of Jesus as uniquely divine is a brilliant conceit—not believable, but brilliant. Jesus is God packaged in individual form for individual consumption. And especially in Western culture, the individual is the basic unit of exchange. People vote as individuals in order to govern themselves: that's democracy. People own the fruits of their labor as individuals: that's capitalism. People confess their sins as individuals in order to receive salvation: that's Christianity. Judaism and Islam are similar in this respect. Most Westerners who reject religion place even more emphasis on the individual than those who don't. It's no surprise, then, that people in the West seek a God to whom they can relate as individuals.

But God doesn't have to be a person-like being for us to take the experience of God personally. Our experience of beauty, for example, can be intensely personal—even if there's not a person in sight. We can feel soothed by the sight of a mirror-calm lake, or inspired by the sound of a thunderous waterfall, or diminished by the sound of a powerful thunderstorm. The same is true of our experience of God. God can be deeply felt, even if the experience isn't directly mediated by a person-like presence.

On the other hand, sometimes the experience has a distinctly personal quality. Recall the words of Schleiermacher, now applied to our experience of God: our experience of being connected to everything that is—all that is present, as well as all that is past, and all that is possible: "At this moment I am its soul, for I feel all its powers and its infinite life as my own; at that moment it is my body, for I penetrate its muscles and its limbs as my own, and its innermost nerves move according to my sense and my presentiment as my own."

If you find yourself feeling despondent or discouraged, remember all that is past. Call to mind people from your own life who are gone now or people from ages past who showed the kind of pluck or resilience that you could use now. In his letter to the Hebrews (12:1), the Apostle Paul spoke of a great "cloud of witnesses" that encompass us and help us stay the course. Taken together, the people who have walked these paths before us can provide powerful inspiration. As Schleiermacher reminds us, we can feel all their powers and infinite lives as our own.

This reminder is more than mere metaphor. When I'm faced with a mundane task or a commonplace duty, I sometimes think of my paternal grandmother, a diminutive and sometimes dour woman named Lulu. She wasn't a people person by any measure.

But Grandma had a way with paste wax. Raised poor during the Great Depression, she provided safe haven for broken toys and disused household items of every kind. Whatever else they needed in the way of repair, these rescued rejects invariably needed a coat of wax—to make them more beautiful, she always said. Grandma may not have had an ear for conversation, but she had an eye for beauty. She worked hard to leave her corner of the world a little more usable and a little more beautiful.

Though Grandma is long dead, I feel her power and life as my own. The same is true of Schuyler Chapin, a Navy pilot who never attended college, but went on to become general manager of the Metropolitan Opera, then dean of the School of the Arts at Columbia University, and Commissioner of Cultural Affairs for New York City. Whenever I feel ill-equipped and ill-prepared, I remember how far Schuyler went on his durable blend of panache and perseverance. When I think of him, I feel his power and life as my own. The consequent nature of God gathers up all that is past and holds it securely—for me and for you.

The same is true of the future. No matter how dire your circumstances or how dim your prospects, you have a universe of possibilities before you. No matter how badly you failed today, the sun will rise tomorrow to give you another chance. The bluebirds will sing to cheer you up, the black-eyed Susans will shake their sassy heads to provoke a smile, and the wind will tousle your hair to remind you not to take yourself too seriously. Someone you don't even know yet will show up to lend a hand. If you try to go it alone, everything will feel difficult, and nothing will seem possible. But if you open yourself to the possibilities before you, anything can happen, and something will.

When I say I believe in God, I'm saying that I believe in an experience that transcends myself in this place and this moment. I believe in an experience that intimately and extensively connects me to all that is—all that is present, as well as all that is past, and all that is possible. It's the biggest conceivable experience—than which none greater can be conceived, to paraphrase Anselm—well worthy of being called divine.

If you look at the relationship from the divine perspective, however, you can see that we play a vital role as well. Recall that the consequent nature of God is constituted in part by our experience as human beings. The only way God plays an active role in time is through us. Consciousness and choice enter the divine picture through us—through our consciousness and our choices.

To say that we are the presence of God in this world is not a metaphor. We are the face of God in this world, and God's voice and hands. God changes outcomes in this world only as we change them. God is not an independent agent, in other words. God is dependent upon us. The active agency of the divine life emerges through our choices and actions.

This understanding of God is hard to accept—but not because it requires us to believe something miraculous about God. Rather, it requires us to believe something astounding about ourselves: that we are the divine in human form. As such, we bear the burden of the past and offer the optimism of the possible. Only we can extend the arms of refuge and sound the voice of hope. The God of all that is past and all that is possible—our source and destiny—is a God we can believe in.

Several years ago, I preached a sermon at All Souls titled "A God We Can Believe In." I received an e-mail the following day from a member of the congregation. She wrote, "This was a profoundly important sermon for me, and I thank you. Your characterization of God as analogous to beauty, 'needing to be made manifest through other forms as a quality of our experience,' and your reference to Alfred North Whitehead's notion of God as the consequence of experience, and your suggestion that this gives meaning to the child left to die in the elements and to each of us in our darkest moments, are an important shift from the notions I absorbed in my childhood. And your suggestion that all humanity is the vessel of God, the face and hands of God in this world, past and future, suddenly invests our actions with frightening and boundless meaning."

The experience of the God we can believe in—God, revised—can at times be frightening because of our sense of responsibility. But the experience can be boundless as well because of our sense of possibility. To be sure, God cannot be placed under a microscope or subjected to double-blind studies. Nor will God ensure that good things always happen to good people.

But I believe the experience of God is both philosophically necessary and theologically sound. It enables us to interpret our experience and account for its meaning. Faith in God is faith that our experiences, however difficult or sublime, have genuine and abiding significance. It is also faith that the tale of the future has not yet been told—that a night of distress may yet turn into a morning of light.

**CHAPTER 5**

# Who We Are

## *The Human Challenge*

I f you want to live a fulfilling life, you need to believe in a revised God and practice an enlightened form of religion—especially in the modern world. That's the main assertion of this book. The question is why: what's the problem that belief in God and the practice of religion will solve that cannot be solved any other way? Do we as human beings have a problem? Do we need saving? If so, from what? What is the problem to which a political, or social, or psychological solution is insufficient, one that only belief in God and the practice of religion can resolve?

The traditional religious answer is that we need saving because we are sinners. The underlying dynamic of human history, in this view, pits divine forces that would save us against evil forces that would destroy us. The Rolling Stones' classic song "Sympathy for the Devil," sung with appropriate irony and defiance by Mick Jagger, begins with an overture from Lucifer, who says he has been around for eons, stealing souls and filching faith.

The song goes on to chronicle a number of Lucifer's greatest hits throughout human history: religious wars and world wars, assassinations and betrayals and genocide. The song then turns to the question of why Lucifer would conspire to steal faith and engineer mayhem. The answer is that Lucifer turns the moral universe upside down: makes saints into sinners and cops into criminals. Occasionally, just for the thrill of it, he does the opposite and allows bad people to become good. Lucifer is a moral dissembler who ensures that whatever is supposed to happen doesn't.

The song doesn't address the question of who or what might restrain Lucifer because Mick Jagger and Keith Richards, who wrote the song, assumed their fans already knew the traditional answer: God.

In biblical terms, human history provides the backdrop for a cosmic battle between God and the devil. God seeks to save people for an eternity in heaven, while the devil tries to lure people to an eternity in hell.

The idea of human history as an earthly battleground for the cosmic competition between God and Lucifer (who is sometimes called Satan) remains firmly entrenched in the contemporary imagination. The wildly popular Left Behind series of sixteen apocalyptic novels written by Tim LaHaye and Jerry Jenkins between 1995 and 2007 has sold more than 65 million copies to date. In 1998, the first four books in the series simultaneously held the top four places on *The New York Times* bestseller list.

Unlike the Harry Potter series, which even its most fervent fans understand to be an allegory, the authors and most of the readers of the Left B described in the books with the armies of heav ke the righteous with hi Readers who get this no st as their savior straight ey won't be left behind.

The d Satan supposedly too n story from the book o g an apple from the Tre disobedience is prompt rm of a talking serpent. God promptly expels Adam and Eve from the garden, a consequence that signifies their fall from primordial innocence into a state of permanent sinfulness.

To clarify a point that people often get confused about, the sin described in the story had nothing to do with sex—despite the present of ample sexual imagery (nakedness, orb-shaped fruit, a serpent, etc.).

The sin was disobedience: God said not to do something, but Adam and Eve did it anyway. As we will discuss in due course, however, the gender issues present in the Garden of Eden have persisted throughout human history. And it's also worth noting that the primordial sin of humanity, the desire to know the difference between good and evil, is a sin more people should have committed ever since.

The story of the fall also introduced a distinction—much discussed by later writers, in both the Bible and elsewhere—between the state of sinfulness and specific sinful acts. The state of sin into which Adam and Eve fell supposedly separated them from the goodness of God; being sinful in this sense meant being separated from God. This state was induced by a specific act of sin: eating an apple from the forbidden tree.

The question the story doesn't answer is how far Adam and Eve fell. For Adam and Eve's children and for subsequent generations of human beings, did human sinfulness make acts of sin possible or did it make them necessary? In the wake of the fall, are we free to choose between sinful and virtuous acts, or has humanity fallen so far that we are doomed always to sin?

In the centuries between the Genesis account and the birth of Jesus, Jewish rabbis wrestled with this question, according to Elaine Pagels in her book *Adam, Eve, and the Serpent.* The rabbis knew from the creation account, as Pagels tells the story, that God had created humanity in the divine image. Any creature that reflects the image of God, they reasoned, must have its own inherent dignity. The rabbis also knew that God had given men (and, some thought, women as well) the right to rule over the earth. Human dignity, therefore, must be like the dignity ascribed to a sovereign ruler; it acknowledges a source of moral freedom. Thus, the rabbis concluded, human beings are capable of governing not only plants and animals, but themselves as well.

During the first three centuries after Jesus's death, most Christian leaders followed the rabbinic approach. Gregory of Nyssa, a fourth-century Christian bishop in Armenia, expressed our human capacity for governing our own actions in this way: "The soul...is governed and ruled autonomously by its own will" (Pagels, p. 73).

In the late fourth and early fifth centuries, however, a Christian convert from Roman North Africa named Augustine of Hippo mapped out a radically different approach. Instead of continuing the rabbinic emphasis on original human dignity and freedom of the will, Pagels explains, Augustine insisted that humanity had been irreparably damaged by the fall. Because of that "original sin," he believed humanity had been rendered sick, miserable, and hopelessly enslaved to sin.

Why did Augustine conclude that humanity had lost its capacity to govern its own actions? The answer is curiously narcissistic: because he was unable to exert rational control over his own sexual impulses. "In the sixteenth year of the age of my flesh," Augustine writes in his *Confessions*, "the madness of raging lust exercised its supreme dominion over me" (Pagels, p. 105). Augustine felt powerless, captive and victim of demons within. Over time, Augustine came to believe that spontaneous sexual desire was proof that original sin had implicated the entire human race.

The story of how this view came to dominate Western Christianity is a disturbing tale. Elaine Pagels tells it brilliantly, although she finds it hard to believe that thoughtful people were taken in by Augustine's argument. One reason for its eventual success, she says, was that it justified the authority of the church and the state. By insisting that humanity, ravaged by sin, now lies helplessly in need of outside intervention, Augustine's theory justified the imposition of church authority—by force, if necessary—as essential for human salvation. It also justified the use of state power to enforce the soul-saving dictates of the church.

This doctrinal endorsement of coercive church and state power inevitably led to horrors like the Crusades and the Inquisition, among others (pp. 118–119).

The key question for us, however, is not whether destructive impulses or pernicious addictions sometimes overtake and overwhelm us. But is the human condition such that we are, in the words of the Hebrew prophet Jeremiah, "deceitful above all things, and desperately wicked?" (17:9, King James Version).

Admittedly, there's no shortage of evidence that human beings are sometimes sinful and wicked, even depraved. As the Smashing Pumpkins memorably put it in their song "Bullet with Butterfly Wings," which won a Grammy Award in 1997, "The world is a vampire." A father kills his daughters in Pakistan for leaving home with a non-relative, village men stone a woman in Afghanistan for having been raped by one of the men in the village, a gunman opens fire in a crowded movie theater in Colorado, or in a Sikh temple in Wisconsin, or in an elementary school in Connecticut: the list of atrocities that suck civilization out of society could go on and on.

Even so, original sin is a hard doctrine to believe in. History demonstrates that fervent believers sometimes have an appalling capacity to commit horrible acts, while unbelievers often act with deep compassion. On empirical terms, a diagnosis of original sin doesn't fit the evidence.

The doctrine also fails on logical grounds. It's based on the belief that Adam and Eve—the first human beings—were created without sin in God's perfect image, but fell from God's favor when they sinned in the Garden of Eden. Since that moment of original sin, the story goes, God has searched for a way to enable men and women to redeem themselves and reclaim their original perfection. At various points in human history, God sent commandments to guide the people, prophets to warn them, plagues to punish them, and even oppressors to haul them off into captivity, but nothing seemed to work.

Finally, with the eternal destiny of humanity hanging in the balance, God came to Earth and took on a human body. The Christian word for this event is incarnation, which comes from Latin roots meaning "to become flesh." The goal of the incarnation was for this God in human form to live a perfect life and die a perfect death, which would satisfy the requirements of divine justice by paying the penalty incurred by all who had sinned. Men and women throughout time and history would thereby be rescued from eternal damnation.

One crucial element in this salvation story has to do with the birth of Jesus. The doctrine of the virgin birth holds that Mary conceived and gave birth to Jesus while remaining a virgin. The biblical account says that Mary was "found to be with child from the Holy Spirit" (Matthew 1:18). If Jesus had been conceived in the usual way, he supposedly would have inherited the original sin bequeathed to all human beings by Adam and Eve's transgression in the Garden of Eden. In that case, Jesus could not have lived a perfect life and died a blameless death, which most Christians believe he needed to do in order to pay the debt for all human sin.

I should note that it was Mary's supposed virginity that supposedly safeguarded Jesus from the stain of original sin. In other words, original sin gets transmitted through the male, not the female. The Roman Catholic doctrine of the immaculate conception employs additional protections by insisting that Mary herself, though born of two human parents in the usual way, was conceived immaculately, that is, without original sin infecting her. In any event, Joseph's involvement would have doomed the entire enterprise. Coming from such relentlessly patriarchal religions (Islam also subscribes to the virgin birth, though Judaism obviously does not), this represents a remarkable, if inadvertent, moment of doctrinal truth-telling.

While the virgin birth may aptly symbolize how powerfully Christians believe the divine was present in Jesus, let's not mince words:

it didn't happen. Even if we ignore the need for magic, the story doesn't hold up on literary grounds either. The New Testament stories about Mary and the birth of Jesus that were written in the several decades after Jesus died make no mention of the virgin birth. The references to the virgin birth that do appear in the New Testament were written or added up to a century later, echoing the virgin birth myths that were common in the ancient world.

Yet contemporary belief in the historical veracity of the virgin birth persists. According to a 2009 Harris Poll, Americans are more likely to believe in the virgin birth (61 percent) than they are to believe in evolution (45 percent). A poll cited by Nicholas Kristof in his August 15, 2003 column in *The New York Times* found that 91 percent of American Christians believe in the virgin birth, as do 47 percent of non-Christians.

I'm aghast at these numbers. They suggest that most Americans have not tried to reconcile the actual world we live in with the alternate world of ancient mythology. It's bad enough that people who've been to school for a dozen years or more, own Smartphones, travel in airplanes, and get regular vaccinations would believe such a thing. What's worse is that they believe this act of divine insemination would solve humanity's most fundamental problem, which it won't. But as long as people think it will, they are unlikely to address the real problem facing humanity, which we'll address shortly.

But first, let's look at what typically happens when people take measure of the biblical tradition and find it wanting, at least as a guide to life in the modern world. The doctrines of the fall and the virgin birth aren't outliers in the tradition. They aren't the crazy uncle and crotchety grandfather in a family that's otherwise easy to live with. The biblical tradition constructs an alternate universe—a way of believing and living that, in significant ways, stands at odds with what we know to be true and what enables human beings to flourish.

Does this alternate universe hang together? Yes, but it's a fundamentally different reality from the one most of us—even the most devout believers in traditional religion—occupy most of the time. My goal is to encourage people to reconcile the universe of their beliefs about religion with the universe of their beliefs about everything else.

More and more people are deciding the world of the Bible isn't a world they can inhabit. When this happens, they often strike out on their own, relieved to be free of the constraints of organized religion. In *Restless Souls: The Making of American Spirituality from Emerson to Oprah*, the Princeton historian Leigh Eric Schmidt observes that countless American churchgoers have rejected their inherited faith traditions and become what Schmidt calls spiritual seekers, turning to individualized sources of enlightenment. In other words, they become spiritual rather than religious.

This trend is not a new feature of American religious life, according to Schmidt. We did not discover spirituality for the first time during the psychedelic days of the 1960s, nor did we first notice mysticism when Madonna took up Kabbalah, a form of ancient Jewish mysticism. Pro basketball coach Phil Jackson was not the first American to find Buddhism enlightening, nor did Oprah pioneer the idea that spirituality involves feeling good about ourselves. The penchant for being spiritual Lone Rangers has been part of our national character from the very beginning. We have always been a nation of individual seekers (Schmidt, pp. 1–23).

This individualist approach to spirituality, Schmidt notes, was sufficiently well established, and sufficiently worrisome, that the French journalist Alexis de Tocqueville, who visited American for the first time in the 1830s, expressed his concern about it. America is a "novel expression" of individualism, Tocqueville said. When it comes to religion, however, the new democracy seems to throw each of its citizens "back forever upon himself alone" and "to confine him entirely within the solitude of his own heart" (Schmidt, p. 70).

One of the quotes included by Schmidt on the faceplate of his book comes from the historian John Weiss, who succinctly summarized this individualist approach in his 1871 book *American Religion*: "America is an opportunity to make a Religion out of the sacredness of the individual."

A key catalyst in this move to individualize spirituality was the transcendentalist movement, which launches Schmidt's account and plays a leading role in my own tradition. An influential movement of the early nineteenth century, transcendentalism was led by Ralph Waldo Emerson, Margaret Fuller, and Henry David Thoreau—all Unitarians. While Emerson and Thoreau are better known, Fuller was at least their intellectual peer; in her own mind, she was their superior. For several years, Fuller served as editor and one of the main writers for the *Dial*, the influential journal of the transcendentalist movement. Her major work, *Woman in the Nineteenth Century*, was published in 1845 and became the guide star of the women's rights movement that began three years later.

The transcendentalists insisted on the sanctity and agency of the individual, especially individual women. As Margaret Fuller said of marriage, "We must have units before we can have unions" (p. 89). From this perspective, the transcendentalists emphasized three main ideas: the divinity of nature, the worth of the individual, and the capacity of each person to know the truth directly. By "directly," the transcendentalists meant without the intermediary of scripture, doctrine, or church. "The stern old faiths have all pulverized," Emerson insisted in his essay "Worship" in *The Conduct of Life*. " 'Tis a whole population of gentlemen and ladies out in search of religions" (p. 882).

In 1838, Emerson gave an address to the seniors graduating from the Divinity School at Harvard, his alma mater. In the speech, Emerson sought to identify the causes of what he called "a decaying church and a wasting unbelief." Because Christianity had focused on the divine nature of Jesus and neglected the moral nature of humanity, he said, true worship had departed from the church, and thus the edifications of worship had been lost altogether.

As a result, Emerson lamented, "Then all things go to decay. Genius leaves the temple, to haunt the senate, or the market. Literature becomes frivolous. Science is cold. The eye of youth is not lighted by the hope of other worlds, and age is without honor." What can be done about this wasting away? Emerson responded, "The remedy is already declared in the ground of our complaint of the Church. We have contrasted the Church with the Soul. In the soul, then, let the redemption be sought" (pp. 87–88).

By rejecting the church out of hand, Emerson sought a direct and immediate experience of God; he wanted his own revelation. Emerson believed the soul of each individual is identical with the soul of the world and contains what the world contains. He begins his essay "Nature" by asking: "Why should not we [as individuals] also enjoy an *original relation to the universe* . . . . Why should we grope among the dry bones of the past?" (p. 7). His doctrines of self-sufficiency and self-reliance assert that we as individuals must have the courage to trust our intuition as we live according to the universal moral laws we intuitively perceive.

One of Emerson's most vocal critics in his own day was Henry Whitney Bellows, who was minister of All Souls in Manhattan (where I now serve as minister) from 1839 to 1882. In 1859, two decades after Emerson's Divinity School address (Bellows had been a student there at the time), Bellows himself gave an equally momentous address at Harvard. He said that the church was not dispensable at all, but rather was a divine, necessary, and permanent institution, like the family and the state.

In the years following his address, Bellows imagined a church that could respond to the challenge of the Enlightenment. Enlightenment thinkers had rejected the ultimate authority of the Bible and the church and instead had embraced human reason and experience. The church

Bellows imagined would respond to this challenge without becoming rigidly dogmatic, like the fire and brimstone preachers of the Great Awakening, or becoming completely lifeless, as Emerson charged.

Bellows did not take up deism—the faith of many Enlightenment thinkers—but continued to identify himself as a Unitarian Christian: he believed in the teachings of Jesus but not in his divinity. Bellows recognized, however, that the church needed to be reanimated by this new spirit of inquiry. He had in mind what Thomas Jefferson had taken for granted half a century before: the Unitarian faith would become the leading faith of our nation. Bellows explained, "My theory of the National Church of America is the old church inspired with the new liberty and motion of life." He defined this church as one that would allow "the fresh air of intellectual liberty to blow in at the doors, and the present lights of science and experience to shine in at its windows." It would be "worshipful and tender, humane and devout, tolerant yet earnest; in short a Church in which the open avowed Creed should be in congruity with men's opinions on other subjects: science, politics, art, business, pleasure, and this life's honest legitimate concerns" (Kring, *Henry Whitney Bellows*, pp. 191–196, 306–307).

Neither Jefferson's vision nor Bellow's dream of an enlightened church came to pass. In the wake of the Civil War, the divide between defenders of traditional religion (especially the preachers of the Second Great Awakening) and those who championed an individualist approach to spirituality continued to widen. But the underlying question of what eventually happens to individuals who have been loosed from their doctrinal shackles persisted.

Thomas Hardy's 1895 novel *Jude the Obscure* sounds a cautionary note about the perils of freedom. As Hardy tells the story, Jude lives in the small English village of Marygreen, which stands a short journey outside the cathedral and university city of Christminster, a city not unlike Oxford or Cambridge. Times were changing at Marygreen, for Jude and for everyone else. The institutions on which life had always rested were collapsing. The schoolmaster was leaving the village for a better post in Christminster, and his students didn't know where to turn. The rector of the village church was away too. In fact, the original church had been torn down and its materials used for pigsty walls and garden seats. The design of the new church was modern and unfamiliar. In the face of these changes, Hardy says, "everybody seemed sorry" (p. 3).

On the one hand, these changes symbolize a new era of opportunity for Jude and Sue, the young woman who eventually becomes his wife. Sue is told at one point, "You are free, absolutely; and your course is your own" (p. 245). The slate of old ways and old institutions has been wiped clean.

But as the old order breaks into fragments, Sue and Jude find themselves caught between two worlds, between an old world in which everyone is given a place by society and a new world where individuals define themselves in their own eyes. It is a challenge they try desperately to meet.

Early on, Jude tries to find either in his new place in Christminster or in his relationship with Sue a means of resolving his crisis of meaning. Hardy tells us: "It had been the yearning of his heart to find something to anchor on, to cling to" (p. 21). But Jude would never find what he sought: he would never find something to anchor on. The chaos of change frightened him, and his lack of courage kept him from discovering where he fit in the new world that was emerging.

Near the end of the novel, surrounded by the fearful wreckage of their lives—divorces, dead children, failed vocations—Jude and Sue hold each other close with a sadness that offers neither the redemption of tragedy nor the relief of resignation. They tried to build a new world for themselves, but too late they discover that they do not know how, nor can they reconstruct the old. In the end, Jude is dead.

During the time Hardy was writing *Jude the Obscure*, the Norwegian Expressionist Edvard Munch was painting his famous work *The Scream*.

Thomas Hoving, longtime director of the Metropolitan Museum of Art in New York City, believes *The Scream* is one of Western civilization's greatest works of art. Munch's harshly colored painting, surreal in both tone and form, depicts a person standing alongside a railing, against the backdrop of a foreboding landscape and turbulent sky. With hands over ears and mouth open in a tormented scream, the person appears to be in existential agony.

Before Munch, Hoving says, human fear and pain were portrayed by specific depictions of events such as epic battles, hand-to-hand combat, the torturing of saints, or people being attacked by fierce animals. Some of these classic portrayals are indeed frightening, but they are not as frightening as Munch's image of psychological fear.

Yet nothing in Munch's landscape portends a sense of horror. The sunset may look odd, but "it's not the end of the world, nor the advent of a holocaust, nor the beginning of a disastrous war. Or is it all of these? That's why *The Scream* works so well. Its power lies in the peacefulness of its setting and the absence of anything at all to be afraid of" (Hoving, p. 64).

Another quality of this painting heightens the sense of foreboding even further: the screaming person stands alone. The two other people in the picture stand at a distance, aloof, unmoved by the anguished cry of the person before them. No matter what prompted the scream, and no matter what consequences follow, suffering happens alone.

In retrospect, *The Scream* seems an appropriate introduction to the twentieth century. After an initial world war, a great depression, and a second world war, Paul Tillich described the postwar era in America and Europe as an "age of anxiety." Perhaps the leading Protestant theologian of the twentieth century, Tillich noted that the century had witnessed remarkable achievements along with terrible devastation. Western civilization, he said, had experienced the breakdown of religious and political absolutism and the development of liberalism and democracy, along with the rise of a technical civilization that had triumphed over its enemies.

Along the way, however, the modern world had lost a spiritual center that could provide answers to the questions of the meaning of life. Humanity was now free to live without reference to God. But freedom brought with it overwhelming responsibility and the eternal threat of what Tillich termed "non-being," which was his way of referring to the loss not only of meaning, but of existence itself.

Freedom produced anxiety in all directions. For many people, Tillich said, the crisis of meaning had "the character both of a trap without exit and of an empty, dark, and unknown void" (p. 63). Humanity's astounding technological achievements now included the ability to annihilate itself. It was an age of anxiety.

Psychiatrist Victor Frankl's book titled *Man's Search for Meaning* was another best-selling chronicle of the age of anxiety. During the Holocaust, Frankl had worked over a period of several years in four different concentration camps. Based on those experiences, he described the emptiness that remains after the loss of meaning as an existential vacuum. Writing in the 1950s, Frankl observed:

*The existential vacuum is a widespread phenomenon of the twentieth century. This is understandable; it may be due to a twofold loss which man has had to undergo since he became a truly human being. At the beginning of human history, man lost some of the basic animal instincts in which an animal's behavior is embedded and by which it is secured. Such security, like Paradise, is closed to man forever; man has to make choices. In addition to this, however, man has suffered another loss in his more recent development inasmuch as the traditions which buttressed his behavior are rapidly diminishing. No instinct tells him what he has to do and no tradition tells him what he ought to do; sometimes he does not even know what he wishes to do. Instead, he either wishes to do*

*what other people do (conformism) or he does what other people wish*
*him to do (totalitarianism). (p. 106)*

Frankl goes on to say that the experience of living in an existential
vacuum mainly manifests itself in boredom and apathy. While boredom indicates a loss of interest in the world, Frankl says, apathy betrays
a lack of initiative to do something in the world, to change something
in the world.

Fifty years later, Frankl's astute analysis of his time has become
inadequate for ours, though people today still reveal a deep-seated
need to either do what everyone else is doing, however meaningless,
or do what they're told, however ill-advised. Even so, the existential
vacuum of the 1950s has been replaced by the existential overload of
the twenty-first century. If anything, the world today is too much
with us. More than anything, we feel overwhelmed, and we've become
jaded in response. Skepticism has replaced boredom, and cynicism has
replaced apathy as the dominant spiritual traits of our time.

In the meantime, our spiritual hunger continues to deepen. We are
more connected than ever and also more lonely. We accomplish more,
but with less satisfaction. We live more rapidly, but fewer experiences
endure. We feel lost in a world teeming with facts and alone in a world
teeming with people.

One of the most profound depictions of our existential reality today
comes from Green Day, a band that came out of the punk clubs of the
San Francisco Bay area in the late 1980s. Their album *American Idiot*
was the third-best–selling album of 2005. Like Green Day's previous
albums, *American Idiot* is fueled by two passions: a deep-rooted aversion
to authority and a deep-seated sympathy for outcasts.

In common usage, the word "idiot" means a person who is foolish or stupid. In fact, the word actually means a person who is ignorant. But the original meaning of the word "idiot" comes from the
ancient Greek word *idios*, which means "one's own" or "private." In

this sense, the true meaning of the album title *American Idiot* appears in the song "Boulevard of Broken Dreams," the ballad that won the Grammy Award in 2006 for best record. The song chronicles the life of a solitary seeker who walks alone.

Our emancipation from the narrow orthodoxies of the stern old faiths gives us freedom to explore new and diverse spiritual lands. But the road of the private seeker is a lonely road because only one person is on it. The road can swiftly become a boulevard of broken dreams.

When people learn that I don't believe in a supernatural God, they sometimes wonder why I'm a minister. I suggest that they watch the music video of "Boulevard of Broken Dreams," and then I tell them where I believe the boulevard of broken dreams ends. As individuals, we need to be free, but we also need to belong.

To what do we need to belong? In chapter two, we examined Walt Whitman's celebrated poem "Song of Myself," in which he says that he is made of atoms. He refers to himself as "Walt Whitman, a kosmos," and says that "every atom belonging to me as good belongs to you." Whitman insists that the self exists in a system where everyone is who they are by virtue of their relationships to everyone and everything else.

My identity is principally defined not by freedom but by relationships. Who am I? A collection of more atoms than you can imagine and more relationships than you can count. If you trace my atoms all the way back in time and my relationships all the way out in space, you will eventually account for everything in the universe. If you look ahead into my future, you'll encounter all the possibilities that could conceivably arise from the circumstances of my present.

As human beings, we are constituted by our connections to the people and the world around us: we belong to everything. If we don't belong, then we don't exist. In fact, the essence of life is not freedom, but its opposite: dependence. We depend upon the world around us for oxygen to breathe, for water to drink, and for food to eat. We depend on parents to conceive us, teachers to teach us, friends to befriend us, lovers to love us, physicians to heal us, and so on. For everything whatsoever, from molecules to galaxies, the first principle of existence is not independence, but rather utter dependence. We owe our very existence to sources formed by a history we cannot control; our destiny extends beyond a horizon we cannot imagine. If utter dependence is the first principle of the universe, and I believe it is, then the most profound human error—the fundamental human sin—is to live as though we're not dependent.

Several years ago, I preached a sermon on this topic, and a woman came up to me afterward and challenged me on this point. "You're not describing my experience as a woman," she said. "I'm stuck at home with the kids, almost completely dependent upon my husband. I wish I had the problem you're describing. I wish I could live as though I'm not dependent. I'd love to be a sinner in that sense."

Her response pulled me up short and caused me to examine more carefully what I mean by dependence in general and utter dependence in particular. Irene P. Stiver, in her essay "The Meanings of 'Dependency' in Female-Male Relationships" (in *Women's Growth in Connection*), asks why both women and men tend to view dependency in pejorative terms. Drawing on the work of Carol Gilligan and others, Stiver observes that "men see dangers more often in close personal affiliations than in achievement, and they construe danger to arrive from intimacy. Women, on the other hand, perceive danger in impersonal, achievement situations and construe danger to derive from competitive success" (pp. 144–145). Men fear being smothered by a relationship or humiliated by rejection or defeat, she says, while women fear isolation—that in being set apart by success, they will be left alone.

In both cases, Stiver goes on to say, fear of dependency in its constructive form—"experiencing oneself as being enhanced and empowered through the very process of counting on others for help"

(p. 160)—shortchanges the experience of both men and women. In general, she concludes, this fear tends to make men wary of intimacy and women wary of success. In her book *The Creation of Patriarchy*, Gerda Lerner quotes Nancy Chodorow, who reaches a similar conclusion: "The basic feminine sense of self is connected to the world; the basic masculine sense of self is separate" (p. 44).

These dynamics have developmental origins. Jean Baker Miller, in her discussion of "The Development of Women's Sense of Self" (also in *Women's Growth in Connection*), recounts the psychoanalytic understanding of how we develop our gender identity. It happens primarily through interaction with our mothers. The strong physical attachment between mother and child—constant in the womb, then intermittent later on—yields a close emotional bond as well.

As we grow older, the situation begins to change. A female child continues to identify with her mother. In other words, she becomes a woman by becoming like her mother. A male child, on the other hand, develops his gender identity by separating himself from his mother, by becoming independent of her support and nurture. In other words, he becomes a man by distancing himself from his mother and all she represents. In the long run, women tend to understand themselves in terms of their relation to those around them; men tend to understand themselves in terms of their difference from those around them.

If I cast these conclusions in geographical terms, men generally view themselves as a success when they stand at the top of the world, while women generally view themselves as a success when they stand at the center of the world. One perspective is about distinction; the other is about relation. Men often view success as something that happens outside of themselves, as a process of distinguishing themselves from others in the field. The problem is that success in this form can never fully come to anyone. Even if one conquers the whole world, what remains is only to weep that there is nothing left to conquer. Many women, as their developmental origins suggest, judge their lives as successful when they have strong, nurturing relationships with significant others in their lives.

In the larger sense, none of us is either wholly masculine or wholly feminine. There are elements of both within each of us, "top of the world" impulses that leave us increasingly isolated and alone, as well as "center of the world" impulses that enable us to develop ever fuller relationships with those around us. Our patriarchal lineage tends to reinforce and reward the former; my intention is to rewrite our understanding of sin and salvation to focus on the latter. At our best, we live not at the top but at the center of the world, in what the poet and essayist Audre Lorde calls a "deeply female and spiritual plane" (p. 53).

This analysis rings true—both in my own personal experience and in my pastoral interactions with men and women over the past twenty years. And I think this analysis is useful, though insufficient, when we talk about dependence in the theological sense. While I think Stiver is mostly right, she ultimately describes dependency as the process "of counting on others for help"—as though such help is somehow optional or ancillary, as though ideally we could get by on our own.

But we can't. In her 2001 essay "Disabled Lives: Who Cares?" in the *New York Review of Books*, the philosopher Martha Nussbaum reviews several books that deal with what she calls extreme dependency: situations in which children or adults have mental, physical, or social disabilities that require extensive and even hourly care from others. She points out that the way we think about the needs of children and adults with disabilities should not be treated as a special department of life, cordoned off from the needs of average people. Quite the contrary: when life as a whole is taken into account, dependency looks more like the rule than the exception. Nussbaum concludes, "As the life span increases, the relative independence many of us enjoy looks more and more like a temporary condition, a phase of life that we move into gradually, and which we all too quickly begin to leave. Even in our prime, many of us encounter shorter or longer periods of extreme dependency on others—after surgery or a severe injury, or during a period of depression or acute mental stress."

Most of us don't want to hear that independence is a temporary condition or that the payoff for being self-reliant is to live in a state of isolation. We would just as soon forget that freedom's just another word for nothing left to lose. We long to be forever young, self-reliant, and independent.

But we can't get by on our own, not ever—hence my theological description of us as being "utterly dependent" upon the people and world around us. The dictionary defines "utter" as "carried to the highest degree" or "absolute." The fear that constitutive relationships will stymie us at work or smother us at home are fears worth taking seriously, but only within the context of ensuring that the relationships upon which we utterly depend for everything are constructive in both directions: both for us and for the people and the world around us.

In his book *Restless Souls*, Schmidt comes around to ask a telling question: "Was the point precisely the *freedom* of spiritual seeking? Or was the real point to find a well-marked path and submit to the disciplines of a new religious authority in order to submerge the self in a larger relationship to God and community? And if one submitted to that kind of regulation, did one forfeit the very liberties—religious and intellectual—to which modern liberal democracy had pledged itself?" (p. 184).

Schmidt presents a false choice, as if we have to choose between religious and intellectual freedom, on the one hand, and submitting to a new religious authority by submerging the self in a larger relationship to God and community, on the other. The truth is that we find freedom through our relationships to the people and the world around us, as well as to all that is past and all that is possible—the experience of God. Any approach to religion that doesn't fully engage the world as we experience it leaves us in dogmatic bondage; any approach to life that doesn't fully acknowledge our dependence leaves us in an existential vacuum. In the modern world, the boulevard of broken dreams ends where the adventure of faith and the practice of a new way of being religious begins.

Over the next several chapters, we'll look at the architecture of transformative dependence, beginning with how enlightened faith connects us to what is possible in our lives and our world and how enlightened religion makes real what is possible. We'll then explore how the discipline of gratitude continually reflects the sources that sustain us and how the ethic of gratitude maps our duty in response. In so doing, we'll discover how to set our sights on ultimate meaning.

## CHAPTER 6

# Keeping the Faith

## *The Necessity of Religion*

that originally meant "unharmed" or "whole." My conversation with a dying woman and her daughter was, in its own way, an attempt to gather up everything that mattered to the three of us and hold it close, even make it whole. The fact that Melissa was dying did not mean Ashlee Simpson was irrelevant to her daughter, nor did Jan's concern about how her hair looked mean that her mother would not die. Nor did the fact that I was the minister mean that I didn't hug my daughter and my wife a little more urgently when I arrived home that evening.

No matter how difficult our circumstances or how dire our situation, we need a way to pull everything together and celebrate wholeness. We need to affirm what is true, cherish what is beautiful, and embrace what is lovely. As we will see, the necessity of religion emerges from this deep-seated and long-standing human need for connection and wholeness.

As an organized way of life, however, religion is on the decline. According to a 2009 *Newsweek* poll, 30 percent of Americans identify themselves as "spiritual but not religious," up from 24 percent in 2005. This open-source approach to spirituality welcomes inspiration wherever it can be found. Perhaps a snippet of Confucius to start the day, a yoga class after work, Gregorian chant as the sun goes down, and a meditation class on the weekend. Religious sampling of this kind certainly adds a patina of spirituality to life, but the question is to what these various spiritual parts, repurposed from diverse religious traditions, add up.

Let's return for a moment to Wittgenstein's analysis of religion. Each religious tradition constitutes a coherent language game: the parts work together in a way that gives believers an overall sense of the meaning and purpose of life. Whether or not a particular religious language game has a foundation in either logic or our experience of the modern world, or both, is another issue. The point is that the beliefs, practices, symbols, and stories make sense within the language game itself.

On this analogy, sprinkling your day with elements from various religious traditions would be like speaking paragraphs in which each sentence is a different language. While this might be fun at cocktail hour, it would make it difficult to communicate anything substantive at other times and places. The experience would be one of those for which "you had to be there." In religious terms, your spiritual experience, when added up over time, would be yours alone.

Many newcomers to All Souls initially enter with the "spiritual but not religious" mantra on their lips. By this I take them to mean that they're looking for something, and they've discovered where they won't find it. Whatever they may mean by "spiritual" (and they mean many different things), they all agree that they won't find it within the bounds of traditional religious—that's the "not religious" part.

What is it that people don't want to be when they want to be "spiritual but not religious"? They don't want to believe something in the absence of evidence that it's true—or even in the face of evidence that it's not. They don't want to reject what they know in deference to a purportedly divine revelation from a supposedly supernatural God. They don't want to champion doctrine that's mired in an antiquated worldview and dogma that's designed to prop up patriarchy. If religion as traditionally practiced were merely irrelevant to life in the modern world, the God wars and doctrinal disputes would subside. But religion has proven hugely destructive in every age, pitting parents against children, neighbors against neighbors, and even nations against nations. Whatever people mean by being spiritual, it's certainly understandable that thoughtful people wouldn't want to be religious.

Even though a substantial portion of the US population today has rejected religion, most of these disaffected souls understand themselves as spiritual, and most seek an experience of the divine. Eric Weiner highlights this quest in an article in *The New York Times* in December 2011, a précis of his book *Man Seeks God: My Flirtations with the Divine.* Weiner notes that while a growing number of Americans are running from organized religion, they are by no means running from God. He calls the religiously unaffiliated—Nones, in current parlance—the undecided of the religious world: drifting and dabbling in everything, searching for a spiritual practice that makes them better, happier people. As for God, Weiner says, wistfully, "We Nones may not believe in God, but we hope to one day. We have a dog in this hunt."

If there is a hymn suitable for those who are spiritual but not religious, it's "I Still Haven't Found What I'm Looking For," by U2, the Bono-led band from Dublin that has become one of the top-selling music artists of all time. The song chronicles a relentless spiritual quest—climbing highest mountains, scaling city walls, speaking with angel tongues, holding the devil's hand—to no avail. In the end, the seeker remains unsatisfied, the quest unfulfilled.

What are we looking for? A way of believing that doesn't require us to believe the unbelievable. A way of living that doesn't require us to do things that seem irrelevant or, even worse, that turn out to be wrong-headed and destructive. We're looking for a God we can believe in and a way of life that unites everything we know and everything we experience. We're looking for a way to pull everything together and celebrate wholeness. Where do we look to find a way of believing and living that fits these requirements?

A little more than a century ago, William James published a series of lectures titled *The Varieties of Religious Experience*, which rightly came in second on the Modern Library's list of the most important nonfiction books of the twentieth century. In his lectures, James introduced a radical new approach to the study of religion. He proceeded not by examining scriptures, dogmas, and other external forms of religion, but by studying the actual experience of religious individuals.

James had two goals, as he explained in a letter to his friend Fanny Morse. The first was to establish that the real backbone of the world's religious life was the experience of the individual believer and not philosophy or doctrine. The second was "to make the hearer or reader believe what I myself invincibly do believe, that although all the special manifestations of religion may have been absurd (I mean its creeds and theories) yet the life of it as a whole is mankind's most important function" (Richardson, p. 391).

Before James, most people failed to make this crucial distinction. Either they accepted religion on its own terms, complete with scriptures, creeds, and dogmas, or they judged the entire enterprise absurd and rejected it completely. James separated what he called the absurd part of religion (the creeds and theories) from the central importance of religion in human experience.

James was part of a group of late nineteenth-century philosophers—Oliver Wendell Holmes and John Dewey among them—who became known as pragmatists. At the time, Darwinism was eroding faith in the Bible as a scientifically and historically accurate text; the pragmatists helped hasten that erosion. They championed the belief that certainty lies within individuals rather than in external things like creeds and scriptures. Instead of bowing to religious dogmatism and scientific orthodoxy, the pragmatists championed open-mindedness and tolerance. They evaluated ideas and values not by assessing who originated them and when, but by their usefulness—their ability to promote happiness, solve problems, and get things done.

William James expanded this principle to include religious beliefs. In his view, true belief is not merely a matter of embracing an authoritative text or adopting an authorized set of doctrines. Rather, it is a way of thinking about life that enables us to make a difference—a positive difference—in the world. If your beliefs cause you to live in ways that make the world a better place, they are true. If not, they are false. The ultimate test of a religious belief is what emerges from the lives of people who believe it. To which I would add one perhaps obvious caveat: your beliefs cannot contravene what we know to be true, either logically or empirically.

Alfred North Whitehead makes the same point in a different way in his book *Religion in the Making*. He points out that believing in religion is not like believing in the facts of arithmetic. People for ages have believed that two plus three equals five. Whenever this belief turns out to be useful—when calculating the number of individuals in a household or the number of dots on a pair of dice—it is applied without question. Everyone accepts the doctrine of addition, and the truth of two plus three equals five does not depend upon who said it or where it first appeared.

Religious belief is a different matter entirely. People have always disagreed about what religion is, or which religious beliefs are valid, or even what it means to say that religion is true. The diversity of opinion has not stopped millions of people from making religious commitments—an unusual situation because we usually avoid making decisions based on information we are not certain about or think may be wrong. If we do not know what 69 times 67 is, for example, we defer any action based on that answer until we find out. With a little effort, we can discover that the answer is 4,623.

The difference between believing in addition and believing in religion, Whitehead goes on to say, is that we *use* arithmetic, but we *are* religious. No one's life has ever been transformed by their faith in the multiplication table. But in some sense or other, transformation is the main function of religion. The point of religious belief is not simply to affirm that something is true. It is to make yourself a better person and your world a better place.

Put differently, the goal of faith is to develop character—to transform our inner life by the force of our beliefs. Whitehead defines religion as "a system of general truths which have the effect of transforming character when they are sincerely held and vividly apprehended." He concludes, "In the long run, your character and your conduct of life depend upon your intimate convictions" (*Religion in the Making*, p. 15).

Within this context, then, what exactly do I mean by faith? Many religious people today view faith as the willingness to believe that sacred scripture—the Bible or the Koran—is a supernatural revelation from God. For them, this kind of faith is a necessary prerequisite to understanding the natural world and human history. As Augustine said in the fourth century, "... believe that thou mayest understand." Children of the Enlightenment seek to move in the opposite direction: not from belief to understanding, but from understanding to belief. We take everything we know into account as we decide what to believe. Enlightened faith never asks us to set aside what we know.

But if our faith is not acceptance of supernatural revelation, what is it? Faith peers into the realm of mystery and transcendence, of meaning and purpose, of value and satisfaction. In the modern world, people of enlightened faith live on the boundary between things we know for certain and things we can never fully comprehend.

For some people, the fact that you can't put faith into a test tube or express religious experience in a formula means that we should keep silent about them. Martha Fay draws the opposite conclusion in her book *Do Children Need Religion?* "Like art and music, religion gives voice to the inexpressible, shape and color to the unseen," she says. "Without its conceits of ritual and symbolism, the insubstantial certainties we all privately harbor are in danger of going unexpressed and unshared" (pp. 124–125).

Because faith stands on the boundary between certainty and mystery, it is always at risk of being either dismissed as irrelevant by scientific certitude or turned demonic by religious orthodoxy. At its best, however, faith is a commitment to live with the belief that life is a wondrous mystery, that love is divine, that we are responsible for the well-being of those around us. Faith is a commitment to live fervently and devoutly, with eyes wide open and mind fully engaged, but also with heart open to mystery and soul attuned to the transcendent.

Faith requires a leap of the moral imagination to connect the world as it is to the world as it might become. As such, faith is not a product of reason, or knowledge, or evidence, or even of experience, though each of these plays an important role in faith. Faith looks at what is and imagines what might be. It requires a leap of the moral imagination to construct a bridge from what is past to what is possible. In this sense, faith is a gift of God—the God we experience as the source of all that is possible.

Let's say you look at your schedule one day and come to the realization that you're spending too much time watching television and not enough time cultivating deep friendships. Or you decide that you should give more money to worthy causes or invest more energy in your marriage or relationship. You commit yourself to making a change. You take the leap. But how can you ensure that you won't fall flat on your face?

The poet Emily Dickinson once described faith as . . .

*. . . the Pierless Bridge*
*Supporting what We see*
*Unto the Scene that We do not—*
*Too slender for the eye*

*It bears the Soul as bold*
*As it were rocked in Steel*
*With Arms of Steel at either side—*

Faith is a leap of the moral imagination. But without something to hold it up, faith will eventually come crashing to the ground. It needs an external means of support: arms of steel on either side.

A couple of years ago, my wife, Holly, and I attended a workshop on the neurobiology of enlightenment led by Gessner Geyer from Harvard. For non-scientists like me, the workshop was a primer on how the human brain works and, more importantly, how it develops and changes. For scientifically well-informed attendees, it was a primer on enlightenment, a term Geyer uses as shorthand for the kind of insight and transformation that we often associate with religious experience. These two areas overlap in an emerging field known as contemplative neuroscience, which integrates brain research with mindfulness meditation.

For our purposes here, the weekend yielded a couple of key insights. One is that our brains are pattern-seeking mechanisms. Whenever possible, our brains revert to established patterns of thought, feeling, and action. To a brain, the old ways are best. It's fiendishly difficult to change entrenched habits and behaviors because we literally have to change our brains to do so—rewire the synapses, create new neural nodes, and establish different pathways. And our brains resist such change, even though we now know that continuing use of ingrained neural patterns allows our brains to atrophy and eventually causes them to shrink.

What causes our brains to thrive? It turns out that change and challenge are the main catalysts for neurological development. Ironically, our brains cannot be changed merely by adding new information or knowledge. What is required is new behavior: a different way of living.

This is where religious disciplines enter the picture. Over the past decade, researchers have been studying people who practice mindfulness, the deep form of awareness developed through disciplines such as meditation and prayer. The researchers have found that mindfulness literally changes the human brain. It is especially effective in developing the brain's capacity for experiencing happiness and fulfillment. In other words, the ancient sages who counseled us to practice the disciplines of attentiveness and gratitude knew what they were talking about after all. Enlightenment isn't the process of learning new ideas; it's the discipline of following a daily spiritual practice.

In order to be effective, however, the discipline must have an objective. The key is to follow rules and commandments not for their own sake, but because they serve a larger purpose. Simply put, faith directs our attention toward that purpose, and religion keeps us focused on it. Faith is a bridge between what is past and what is possible. Religion, in turn, is a way of life that enables our faith to become real. It also carries our faith along from day to day and generation to generation.

Once our moral imagination gives us a glimpse of a different future, we need the endurance to persist until transformation actually happens. Our faith needs an external means of support: stories to restore our courage, symbols to remind us of commitments we have made, and daily rituals to renew our resolve. We need a place to go when we are feeling discouraged and songs to sing when we are full of spirit. We need companions to help bear the load. These supports not only help sustain our faith, but they also help re-create it at other times and places, and for other people.

In my view, the theological term for the supports that sustain and renew our faith is religion. It is the collection of external forms we use—songs, symbols, stories, rituals, obligations, sacred spaces—to carry our faith along from day to day and generation to generation. The meaning of the word "religion" is usually traced to the Latin verb meaning "to bind." Early monastic Christians were called religious because they had taken sacred vows and were bound by solemn orders. This early form of the word religion suggests that religion is a way of life. Faith is a commitment from within that is sustained and renewed by the way of living we call religion. That's why we call it the practice of religion.

Like faith, religion at its best is dynamic and ever changing. It's not a once-and-done collection of songs, symbols, stories, rituals, obligations, and sacred spaces. Just as faith should evolve in response to new knowledge and new experience, so religion should also evolve to adapt to the changing demands of faith and the changing circumstances of the world.

If religion can sustain and renew faith, however, it can also have the opposite effect. The various external forms of religion can become rigid and coercive—an end in themselves. When this happens, religion becomes an obstacle to faith and a barrier against it. For this reason, religion itself must continually be renewed.

The story of a developing religious tradition is the interplay over time of inspiration and transformation. Often, though not always, a founding prophet provides the initial story and substance. As the tradition develops, later interpreters usually expand the message while at the same time sharpening its boundaries. In order to flourish, the tradition must provide its adherents with a way of living that is transformative, meaningful, and satisfying.

At the outset, for example, Christianity was designed for ongoing inspiration and renewal. In his 2007 article "Early Christian Impresarios" in the *New York Review of Books*, Eamon Duffy, a professor of Church History at Cambridge University, points out that early Christianity was more than a new religion. It also brought with it a revolutionary shift in information technology, one that would change its world as profoundly as the Internet has changed ours. Like Judaism and Islam, Christianity is often described as a "religion of the book." This phrase captures the idea of a divinely inspired sacred text that pervades the three religions of Abraham. But it also describes the importance of a material object—a book—in the history and practice of all three traditions.

To us, a book is something printed on both sides of sheets of paper, stitched in bundles between protective covers. But in the ancient world, Duffy notes, a book was a long scroll made of papyrus or parchment. Even today, this is the form in which the books of the Hebrew Bible are read in synagogue worship.

For the people of the ancient world, scrolls symbolized value and permanence. By contrast, flat pages were for writing things that were trivial and ephemeral. Duffy says that students might jot notes on bundles of flat pages, and writers often composed their first drafts on them, but anything of enduring value would be copied onto a scroll.

In fact, our modern book form—known as a codex—evolved from the ancient equivalent of a stenographer's pad. A stack of wooden tablets coated with wax was bundled with string hinges. Information could be jotted onto these tablets with a stylus. When the information was no longer needed, the wax could be heated and smoothed, and the tablets reused. The first books could be recycled in the same way. The bundles of flat pages were written upon with soluble ink that could be washed off and used again. "To inscribe the words of Holy Scripture on such jotting pads," Duffy declares, "would demean its sacred character and authority."

So why did the early Christians deliberately choose the form of the codex rather than the scroll to record their sacred writings? Historians suggest two possible reasons. One may have been to distinguish Christianity in a visual way from its Hebrew origins, like teenagers who dress differently from their parents. The other reason, more intriguing, is that the foundational texts of Christianity were what Duffy calls sacred stenography, a living transcript taken from the testimony of the first witnesses. By placing these statements in codex form, early Christians suggested that the story of their faith was an ongoing chronicle. In the future, the stories and teachings could be amended or perhaps even revised.

Sadly, this paradigm-shattering insight was lost in the eventual battle among Christians to make their scripture just as definitive and unchangeable as a Hebrew scroll. But the insight remains valid. In a changing world, people of authentic faith must keep the book of religion open. The goal is for the form of religion without to enliven the substance of faith within. If the form of religion becomes an end in itself, then faith can easily become demonic.

For people who identify themselves as spiritual but not religious, however, the challenge lies at the other end of the spectrum. They champion faith but dismiss religion—and for good reason. Many people today have given up on organized religion, not only because it has been a hugely divisive and destructive force in human history, but also because it has been painfully destructive in their own lives.

One member of All Souls spoke poignantly from the chancel one Sunday morning about growing up Catholic and discovering that he was gay. He was also left-handed, which the nuns took as a sign that he was evil, possessed by the devil. Eventually he was (literally) beaten into writing with his wrong hand. But the unrelentingly harsh denunciation of his sexual identity drove him from the church; he stayed away for more than two decades. Then, like Melissa and so many others, he found himself in a dark night of the soul. He needed the consolation of faith and the solace of religious community. Fortunately for him, he found All Souls.

If the only church you know is a fortress of dogma and the only god you can conceive of is a supernatural source of caprice and commandments, then away with them. But those aren't the only options. Religion has also been a source of sublime beauty, selfless compassion, and enduring hope. It can be a dynamic incubus of prophetic faith and enduring transformation. Revelation is not sealed; the book of religion must therefore remain open.

For many religions, however, the book of revelation has long been sealed, which is why some religious beliefs and practices today are better than others. The business of comparing religions is fraught with danger, especially since each religion operates in its own linguistic and symbolic world. In her review of Richard Dawkins's book *The God Delusion*, the novelist Marilynne Robinson reminds us of the cautionary note sounded by the nineteenth-century abolitionist and feminist minister Thomas Wentworth Higginson, who insisted that, "in comparing religions, great care must be taken to consider the best elements of one with the best of the other, and the worst with the worst" (p. 84).

This principle does not mean that all convictions and beliefs are thereby equal, however. The commitment to religious pluralism is taken by some to mean that any conviction that is sincerely held is a good conviction, and therefore cannot be criticized or rejected. This is not true. How do we decide which beliefs and commitments are better than others? The test is what goes out from our lives as a result of our faith: the issue of religion.

On these terms, the belief that people who happen to be female are equal in status and role to people who happen to be male is better than the belief that they aren't equal. Beliefs that conform to what reason and experience tell us about ourselves and the world are better than those that don't. Practices that breed bigotry and provoke oppression are worse than those that have the opposite effect. And so on.

In rejecting the God we don't believe in and the practice of a religion we can't abide, it's important to remember that religion must be something in particular. George Santayana once said that the attempt to have a religion without having a particular religion is like trying to speak without speaking a particular language. People who move from one religion to another, he said, often retain what he called a neutral residue of belief, which the traveler may wrongly regard as the essence of all religion.

Yet, upon careful examination, this essence proves to be nothing but the vestige of former beliefs. There is no such thing as religion in general. There are only particular religions, each of which has its own symbols, stories, rituals, and obligations. Every living and healthy religion, Santayana concludes, has its own special and surprising message. "The vistas it opens and the mysteries it propounds are another world to live in; and another world to live in—whether we expect ever to pass wholly into it or not—is what we mean by having a religion" (p. 5).

To state the relationship between spirituality and religion in a different way, if you take yourself seriously as a spiritual person, you'll eventually need to become religious. In his book *Religion for Atheists: A Non-Believer's Guide to the Uses of Religion*, the writer Alain de Botton inadvertently makes this point. Botton insists that the claims of religion are entirely false, yet he readily agrees that religions have important things to teach the secular world. He's not intent on mocking religions like many of his fellow agnostics and atheists. Instead, Botton advises pillaging from religions. They're packed with good ideas on how to live our lives and arrange our societies, he says. Religions can teach us how to build a sense of community, make our relationships last, get more out of art, and overcome feelings of envy and inadequacy.

Botton's goal is to use these religious insights in non-religious ways. He says, "We need institutions to foster and protect those emotions to which we are sincerely inclined but which, without a supporting structure and a system of active reminders, we will be too undisciplined to make time for" (p. 298).

For example, he says art galleries should present paintings not according to period or style, but according to the passions they are likely to evoke. Universities should have departments designed to instill wisdom in students and teach them how to live. Botton also suggests a chain of secular confessionals, which he dubs "talkingcure." And he imagines electronic versions of the Wailing Wall that would anonymously broadcast our inner woes and thereby, he says, "give us all a clearer sense of what is involved in being alive" (p. 191). He wants a chain of Agape restaurants to spring up, where we would eat not with friends but with strangers—the opposite of Facebook.

Botton also wants to build temples for atheists. Why should religions have all the good architecture, he asks? Besides, he adds, the kind of derisive atheism espoused by Richard Dawkins and Christopher Hitchens has not been a constructive force. A series of temples dedicated to positive virtues—love, friendship, or calm—would demonstrate a kinder, gentler atheism. His first monument will be the "Temple to Perspective," a stone tower he hopes to build in the City of London. Its height corresponds to the age of the Earth—one centimeter per million years, with humanity's time on Earth represented by a gold band around the base one millimeter thick.

On the one hand, I agree with almost everything Botton says. On his terms, I'm an atheist too: I don't believe in the God he doesn't believe in either. And I agree that religious practice has practical benefits. On average, people who are religiously active live longer, healthier, and happier lives than people who aren't.

On the other hand, I couldn't disagree with Botton more strongly. He stands in a long line of cynics—Voltaire, Machiavelli, Edward Gibbon, and Jürgen Habermas, among others—who condemn the commitments of religion but embrace, either derisively or wistfully, its effects. Voltaire thought religion was a good way to terrorize the masses into submission.

For his part, Botton is more wistful than most: his face is pressed up against the stained glass window where faith lives and religion gets practiced. He understands the value of religion and sees its benefit. He just doesn't know where to find a temple for the practice of religion that doesn't require him to believe what he knows isn't true.

Like many people today, Botton finds himself fixated on one particular view of God and religion. The religions of the West are based on the belief that God made rules and handed them down to humanity in the form of divine scripture, which directs believers to obey God's commandments. In recent centuries, we've discovered that the universe isn't set up the way our ancestors originally thought. The idea of a supernatural God, like the idea of an Earth-centered universe, must be left behind. This doesn't mean that God doesn't exist or that we don't need to participate in a religious community.

In fact, our need for God and religion is made greater by these discoveries. If God is not supernatural, then religion has a critical role to play. Religion is the process of taking everything we know into account as we forge a life of meaning and purpose. In order to play this role, religion must evolve, and our understanding of God must adapt as well.

To his credit, Botton is trying to respond to this challenge. He knowingly cherry-picks elements of practice from various religions and suggests alternate ways they can be used for individual edification and social benefit. What he hasn't discovered is that the pieces must somehow be put together.

Imagine taking Beethoven's Ninth Symphony and trying to make use of its various elements. The text of the fourth movement—the Ode to Joy—might make a good topic for discussion in a reading group. You could sit alone in the concert hall and marvel at the gold leaf on the ceiling or listen to a clarinetist in the subway play his part of the second movement. You could visit the store where the conductor bought her baton or examine various ways of arranging the instruments on stage. You could study the score or listen to a baritone warm up. You could even hum the Ode to Joy yourself.

All of these elements are crucial to Beethoven's Ninth Symphony. But until they all come together in one place, at one time, in the right way, they don't add up to Beethoven's Ninth. By the same token, religion includes good art and great architecture and stirring music and instructive stories and comforting rituals and prophetic challenges. But until they all fit together in a way that unites spiritual need and moral imagination, they don't add up to transformed lives and a changed world. Religion is an all-or-nothing experience, like Beethoven's Ninth. Religion happens—and transformation comes—within communities of faith, which model for us the fundamental moral truth of the universe: that we are constituted by our relationships and utterly dependent upon them.

For an enlightened religious community, the challenge is to find a middle distance between an individual quest for freedom that leaves us each isolated and an authoritarian insistence on certainty that leaves us all in bondage. We need a way of being religious that sets us free and makes us whole. I believe that the hallmark of this way of being religious is the discipline of gratitude.

## CHAPTER 7

# What We Receive

## *The Discipline of Gratitude*

**Y**ou may agree that we each need to be part of a community, but you may wonder why the community has to be religious. Why can't you join a sports team, or an environmental advocacy group, or even a political campaign? These groups are all united by mutual commitments and shared purposes. Why does the community need to be religious—and what makes it religious? And compared with traditional religious communities, what's the distinctive purpose of a religious community that has evolved to meet the demands of the modern world?

If the fundamental sin of the modern era is the tendency to disregard our utter dependence upon the people and the world around us, then being an integral part of a cohesive community will indeed help solve part of our existential problem. The irony of digital innovation is that we have become increasingly connected to our data but increasingly disconnected from each other. People in our culture today are more isolated and more alone than they have ever been. What's often missing from our digital world is the experience of personal connection and mutual support, of being an individual within a real community.

As the word itself suggests, a community is defined by what the individuals within it have in common. At the top of the All Souls order of service each Sunday stands a quote from William Ellery Channing, whose preaching in New York in 1819 inspired the founding of the congregation. The quote reads: "I am a member of the great family of all souls." For most of us, families provide us with our initial experience of being part of a community. Like all communities, including religious communities, families are defined by shared histories and common rituals.

Some time ago, my wife, Holly, and my daughter, Zoë, and I traveled to Portland, Oregon, for a reunion of Holly's family of origin. Like many families, Holly and her siblings have scattered over a significant swath of the globe: Manhattan, Portland, Anchorage, and Honolulu. Like most contemporary families, the Atkinson clan has been divided by divorce (Holly's parents split up more than thirty years ago, and two of the four siblings, including Holly, have been divorced) and supplemented by subsequent relationships. Some of the supplements showed up in Portland (Zoë and I were there), and others did not (Holly's brother's girlfriend lives on Reunion Island, which lies off Madagascar in the Indian Ocean, and Holly's niece's boyfriend plies a salmon boat in the Bering Sea).

Our gathering reminded me of a poem by Jeredith Merrin, which both lampoons our sometimes convoluted family situations and also states clearly what's missing when we don't have an experience of being deeply connected to the people and world around us. The poem is titled "Family Reunion," and the first part of it reads:

> *The divorced mother and her divorcing*
> *daughter. The about-to-be ex-son-in-law*
> *and the ex-husband's adopted son.*
> *The divorcing daughter's child, who is*
>
> *the step-nephew of the ex-husband's*
> *adopted son. Everyone cordial:*
> *the ex-husband's second wife*
> *friendly to the first wife, warm*
>
> *to the divorcing daughter's child's*
> *great-grandmother, who was herself*
> *long ago divorced. Everyone*
> *grown used to the idea of divorce.*
>
> *Almost everyone has separated*
> *from the landscape of a childhood.*

*Collections of people in cities*
*are divorced from clean air and stars.*

*Toddlers in day care are parted*
*from working parents, schoolchildren*
*from the assumption of unbloodied*
*daylong safety. Old people die apart*

*from all they've gathered over time,*
*and in strange beds. Adults*
*grow estranged from a God*
*evidently divorced from History;*

*most are cut off from their own*
*histories, each of which waits*
*like a child left at day care.*
*What if you turned back for a moment*

*And put your arms around yours? (pp. 3–4)*

Families enable us to put our arms around our histories, sometimes for better and sometimes for worse. Biology and matrimony play a decisive role in creating many families, but what most clearly defines a family over time is its history of shared experiences. Families are constituted by stories, which get endlessly repeated.

Like the day long ago when Holly was driving her mother and younger sister over the Brooklyn Bridge into Manhattan, and Holly's Karmann Ghia burst into flames. We marvel at that story nearly every time we're together—at their good fortune in escaping injury and their good luck in attracting the attention of an Orthodox Jewish man who helped them out.

Or the time when the minister who was to marry Holly's younger sister and her husband in their Michigan home showed up drunk—and four hours late. Granted, they were in the middle of a blizzard at the time, but it turns out he was late mainly because he had been in jail.

Or the time when Holly's brother was showing off his new jet boat at his cabin on a lake in Michigan. He made a right-angle turn at sixty miles an hour and catapulted me—dressed in a heavy wool sweater, corduroys, and boots—into the fifty-degree water, nearly decapitating my young niece as I flew past. Holly was not amused—especially when she learned that her brother had done the same thing to their eighty-five-year-old dad the week before.

Along with stories come family rituals, many of which have to do with food, such as donuts: Doughnut Plant on Grand Street when in New York and Voodoo Donuts on Third Avenue when in Portland. By the way, if you happen to visit Voodoo Donuts, don't be seduced by the Bacon Maple Bar, which sounds good but isn't. Go for the McMinnville Cream instead.

Family traditions develop at the confluence of necessity and nurture. Religious traditions, in contrast, get established when people share a transcendent intention and develop a corresponding way of life. From the perspective of an individual believer, a particular religious tradition usually appears fully developed; a new believer joins a religious family that already has a well-developed history and well-established rituals and obligations, not to mention clearly defined authority structures. In the beginning, however, someone or a group of people had to put the tradition together, usually to carry on the teachings of a charismatic leader, such as Moses (Judaism), Jesus (Christianity), or Mohammed (Islam)—or even Mary Baker Eddy (founder of Christian Science) or Joseph Smith (founder of Mormonism).

Sometimes the process of shaping a new tradition takes centuries, as it did with Judaism and Christianity. In other cases, the process happens much more rapidly, especially when the founder him- or herself

S ome years ago, I made a hospital visit to a woman I'll call Melissa, who had been diagnosed with a relatively rare and extremely aggressive form of cancer. Melissa had come to this country from Malaysia before her then-twelve-year-old daughter, whom I'll call Jan, was born and had raised her as a single parent, without the benefit of extended family. Melissa and Jan had been attending All Souls for about a year.

During my visit, we talked about the challenges Melissa had faced in her life, and especially her frustration that the cancer was not diagnosed earlier. Hers was a story I hear too often, especially from women: her doctors (some of whom were also women) had brushed off her early intimations of trouble. By the time someone started paying attention, it was too late. Within several weeks of my initial hospital visit, Melissa would be dead.

Mostly, we talked about her daughter—about the arrangements she had made for Jan to remain in this country and the hopes she had for her as a young woman. It was a difficult conversation for me, since Jan is about the same age as my daughter Zoë.

Midway through the conversation, Jan walked into the room from one of her first days of the school year. I liked her immediately: strong, smart, and delightfully bold. We talked about the courses she was taking and her new teachers—which ones were on the most sought-after list and which ones were not. We talked about whether her new hairstyle made her face look square (my answer was no). We also discussed whether Ashlee Simpson is musically more talented than her older sister Jessica (my answer was yes).

During that conversation, a line from the poet W. B. Yeats came to mind, in which Yeats speaks of a ceremony of innocence, a word develops the documents—authoritative texts, guides for living—that set the tradition apart. Regardless, someone has to make decisions. What commitments and disciplines do we share in common? What distinguishes us from everyone else?

When people ask me to explain how religions develop, I sometimes suggest that they watch *The Sisterhood of the Traveling Pants*. The movie tells the story of four sixteen-year-old girls, each with an existential crisis too big for her to solve on her own. The girls have been best friends forever, and they aren't pleased about going their separate ways during summer vacation. Bridget, a striking blond athlete, is going to soccer camp in Mexico, where she will try to bury her grief over her mother's suicide by being romantically aggressive toward an off-limits older guy. Lena, who is mostly too serious and shy for her own good, heads for Greece to stay with relatives and finds herself enmeshed in a longstanding family feud. Carmen, the discontented narrator of the tale, embarks to Virginia on a visit to her estranged father, whose abandonment of her years earlier remains a source of deep and searing pain. Tibby, a free-spirited and sarcastic would-be filmmaker, stays behind in Maryland to stock shelves in a Walmart-like department store and work on her documentary about people living lives of quiet desperation. Somewhat by happenstance, Tibby meets a young friend whose personal challenges make Tibby reassess her own narcissism.

Before they part for the summer, the girls go shopping together in a thrift store. They stumble upon a pair of Levis that magically fits each of their various body types perfectly. The friends agree to share the pants all summer long. Each will wear the pants for a week or two, then FedEx the pants to the next girl.

The girls formalize what they come to call the sisterhood of the traveling pants in a ceremony that has many religious features. They meet one night in their own sacred space: a now-unused aerobics studio where their mothers had exercised together during their pregnancies. The girls light candles and form a circle. They spread out their last supper together: raw cookie dough, Pop-Tarts with pink icing, and sour Gummi Worms. Carmen begins: "On the last night before the diaspora, we discovered some magic. Magic comes in many forms. Tonight it comes to us in a pair of pants. I hereby propose that these Pants belong to us equally, that they will travel to all the places we're going, and they will keep us together when we're apart."

Bridget joins in: "Let's take the vow of the traveling Pants," she urges. They each affirm an oath in the flickering candlelight, and then Lena suggests that they should write down some rules, which they do. Not surprising to anyone who's paying attention to the religious potency of this scene, the girls come up with ten rules governing the use of the Pants. The first is that "you must never wash the Pants." The second is that "you must never double-cuff the Pants. It's tacky. There will never be a time when this will not be tacky." And so on, concluding with rule ten: "Remember: Pants = love. Love your pals. Love yourself."

For each of the girls, as Carmen later puts it, "The Pants are like an omen. They stand for the promise we made to one another, that no matter what happens, we stick together. But they stand for a challenge too. It's not enough to stay in Bethesda, Maryland, and hunker down in air-conditioned houses. We promised one another that someday we'd get out into the world and figure some stuff out."

Over the summer, the girls do figure some things out. The summer is a time of both adventure and affliction. But each girl experiences transformation as well, made possible by the Pants, or at least by the presence of the love the Pants represent. Carmen recognizes that the power of the Pants derives from their role as witness: "The Pants were the only witness to all of our lives," she says.

But the Pants do more than just bear witness. At the end of the summer, the girls make inscriptions on the Pants, telling their summer stories with pictures and words that stand out bright against the humble denim. In this way, Carmen says, the Pants are "the witness and the document too"—both revelation and scripture, in other words.

Religious communities help us make sense of our experience against a backdrop of everything else: our own lives and the lives of the people around us, the intriguing yet often perplexing world that surrounds us, the inconceivably vast universe we call home, as well as all that is past and all that is possible. Each religious tradition has a defining discipline: love in the case of Christianity (and the sisterhood), obedience in the case of the Jewish tradition, and submission in the case of Islam. And each tradition has its own set of rules, rites, and obligations, which usually develops in the nascent stage of the tradition to give a strong sense of cohesiveness from within and clear identity from without.

The goal of religion, and the purpose of religious community, is to change what needs changing, to enable us to become better people and the world a better place. Different religions undertake these tasks in different ways. As the sisterhood demonstrates, while the elements of a particular religion must be distinctive, the elements themselves are remarkably arbitrary. For example, one could conceive of a breakaway sisterhood, perhaps developed by several of the girls the following summer, in which double-cuffing was required, not prohibited, and the pants had to be khaki. After all, what sense does it make to wear denim in the summer, especially at the beach?

Because a particular set of rules proves successful in enabling the community to survive and even thrive, the rules can easily come to be seen as necessary in themselves, which they are not, except as they serve to give the community its distinctive identity and practice. Over time, the success of a religious tradition is determined by whether the tradition gives its adherents a sense of identity and purpose, not whether it is logically and empirically well founded. In an ideal case, of course, a tradition would be useful to those within it, as well as reasonable and demonstrably beneficial to those without.

One reason religious traditions can get away with being illogical and historically perverse is that they engage the realm of the transcendent, which is what distinguishes religious communities from other kinds of communities. The word "transcendence" comes from a Latin verb that means "to pass over a physical obstacle, to go beyond a limit, or to climb over the top of a wall or mountain."

In religious terms, transcendence is the ability to go beyond the limited confines of our daily lives and see the reality of the world and our place in it. It's the experience of being burdened by the persistent tragedy of the world and exhilarated by its sublime beauty. Transcendence is the feeling of being deeply connected to everything: all that is present as well as all that is past and all that is possible. The experience of transcendence ushers us into the realm of the divine.

From the perspective of the individual, this experience has a specific character, which Friedrich Schleiermacher highlights in *The Christian Faith*, which you may recall proclaimed that the essence of religion is the feeling of absolute dependence upon God (pp. 16–18). Religion is an experience—a feeling, Schleiermacher called it.

What kind of experience does Schleiermacher have in mind? The religious experience of utter dependence is twofold: a feeling of awe and a feeling of obligation. Both are experiences of transcendence, of being part of something much larger than ourselves. The feeling of awe emerges from experiences of the grandeur of life and the mystery of the divine. It comes when we grasp how insignificant we are when compared to the vastness of the universe, how fleeting and fragile we are when compared to the period and potency of the universe. It comes when we recognize how much we need things we cannot make on our own—the sun, wind, and water; the trees, plants, and animals; even parents, teachers, and friends. This sense of awe and dependence should engender in us a discipline of gratitude, which constantly acknowledges that our present experience depends upon the sources that make it possible.

The feeling of obligation lays claim to us when we sense our duty to the larger life we share. As we glimpse our dependence upon other people and things, we also glimpse our duty to them. This sense of obligation leads to an ethic of gratitude, which takes our experience of transcendence in the present and works toward a future in which all relationships—among humans, as well as between humans and the physical world—are fair, constructive, and beautiful. Again, the reason for religion is the need for transformation.

For members of a particular religious community, the sense of obligation takes a specific form when it comes to their commitment to each other. In the movie *Shall We Dance?*, Richard Gere plays a bored middle-aged attorney who surreptitiously takes up ballroom dancing. His wife, played by Susan Sarandon, becomes suspicious at his renewed energy and vitality. She hires a private detective, who discovers the dance studio and reports the news. She decides to let her husband continue dancing undisturbed.

In the scene where she meets the private detective in a bar to pay his fee and end the investigation, they linger over a drink and discuss why people marry in the first place. The detective, whose countless investigations into infidelity have rendered him cynical about marriage, suggests that the desire to marry has something to do with hormones and passing fancy.

She disagrees. The reason we marry, she insists, is that "we need a witness to our lives. There's a billion people on the planet.... I mean, what does any one life really mean? But in a marriage, you're promising to care about everything. The good things, the bad things, the terrible things, the mundane things...all of it, all of the time, every day. You're saying 'Your life will not go unnoticed because I will notice it. Your life will not go un-witnessed because I will be your witness.'"

The sacramental bond that unites two people in a marriage or committed relationship is known as a covenant. A covenant—the word means mutual agreement—is a promise to bear witness to the life of another: the good things, the bad things, the terrible things, the mundane things.

At its heart, the relationship among members of a religious community is covenantal as well. As with marriage, the relationship also includes other dimensions, such as friendship and perhaps financial and/or legal partnership. But the defining commitment that members of a religious community make to each other arises from their calling—their covenantal duty—to bear witness to each other's lives: the lives they now lead and the lives they hope to lead in the future, and the world they now occupy and the world they hope to occupy in the future.

It's worth remembering that the word "religion" does not mean liberating or setting free, but rather binding together. Religion unites the purpose of our lives as human beings with the purpose that animates the universe. Religion unites the spirit of humanity with the energy that keeps the stars shining, the planets spinning, and the flowers blooming in springtime. Gratitude is the appropriate religious response to our experience of being part of, yet utterly dependent upon, the people around us and the universe that sustains us.

The experience of transcendence is most palpable during worship—the hallmark of a religious community: it's what makes a religious community religious. Worship is an experience in which members of a religious community gather to acknowledge their relationship to each other and to everything else: to all that lies beyond them, and to all that is past and all that is possible. Most of the time, we live with an exceedingly narrow field of view: what's happening in our own bodies, for example, or our own homes, or our own schools or offices, or our own city or nation. In worship, we open ourselves to the widest possible field of view—that field of view wider than which no field of view is possible. At its most poignant and most powerful, worship connects us with everything, from our most hidden heartaches to our most expansive possibilities. In this sense, worship is the wellspring of gratitude, its source and sustainer.

In addition to experiencing a connection to everything we know, worship connects us with what we don't know. Worship is a discipline of opening our hearts to people we don't fully know, our minds to ideas we don't fully comprehend, and our souls to a divine experience we cannot fully name. It reminds us of the ignorance that infuses everything we know and the mystery that lies beyond our understanding.

What happens in worship? Traditions of worship vary widely within and across denominations and religions. Some are informal and casual, or at least appear to be, while others are highly formal and intensely ritualized. Some emphasize ancient teachings and historic rituals, while others employ contemporary stories and music.

As I've noted before, the content of many traditional worship services badly needs to be updated. "Promise me that I'll never again have to recite that creed about Jesus being raised from the dead and seated at the right hand of God the Father," a newcomer to All Souls once challenged me. I promised her that she wouldn't.

"I refuse to go to mosque with my parents anymore," another newcomer confessed to me. "The idea that my wife and I can't worship together, well, it may have made sense once upon a time, but it doesn't make sense in the twenty-first century."

"Why do the scriptures and songs refer only to men—unless they're talking about the Virgin Mary?" another complained of her former congregation. "We can map the human genome, but we can't change 'he' to 'we'?"

In some cases, the problem with traditional worship isn't what's present but what's not. One couple told me that they first came to All Souls a few weeks after the massive earthquake struck Indonesia in December 2004, creating a tsunami that killed more than 200,000 people in eleven countries. The couple went to their previous church the following Sunday, hoping to gain some perspective on this horrible calamity, perhaps even to find some solace. "Not a word about the tsunami," they reported to me. "Nothing in the prayer, nothing in the sermon—nothing at all. As far as the service was concerned, the tsunami never happened."

At its best, worship is the experience of being connected—to our own deepest longings and highest aspirations, to the people and the world around us, to all that is past and all that is possible. In order for this experience to ring true, it needs to resonate with and, hopefully, make sense of the world we actually live in. The elements of an effective worship service need to address four key aspects of human experience: what's true, what's broken, what's right, and what's transcendent.

In worship, we bear witness to what is true. In the Protestant traditions in the United States (which count about half the total population among their adherents), this happens most visibly during the sermon— the sacrament of the word. The theological lineage of the Protestant tradition extends back to the sixteenth-century reformers, who took their liturgical cues from the Christian New Testament, where we read: "In the beginning was the Word, and the Word was with God, and the Word was God" (John 1:1). Because the sacrament of the word is the focus of Protestant worship, the architecture of Protestant churches usually gives prominence to the pulpit.

In contrast, the central sacrament in Catholic and Orthodox liturgies is Holy Communion, also known as the Eucharist, the sacrament of the body and blood of Christ. As recounted in the earliest of the four Gospels, during Jesus's final meal with his disciples on the evening before he died (only much later would it come to be called the Last Supper), Jesus "took a loaf of bread, and after blessing it broke it, gave it to them, and said, 'Take; this is my body.' Then he took a cup, and after giving thanks he gave it to them, and all of them drank from it. He said to them, 'This is my blood of the covenant, which is poured out for many'" (Mark 14:22–24). The Gospel of Luke appends a directive from Jesus: "Do this in remembrance of me" (Luke 22:19). Because of the central role the Eucharist plays in their worship, a central altar typically dominates the sanctuary of Catholic and Orthodox churches.

The scope of what's true for an enlightened community of worshippers includes, well, everything. As we say at All Souls, we gather to contemplate the mystery of God, interpret the wisdom of religion, and explore the insights of science. Our obligation is to bear witness to the truth at its most expansive—the truth as best we can declare it about our lives and our relationships, our aspirations as a religious community and our destiny as a nation, our obligation to the rest of creation and our responsibility to generations who will come after us. In worship, we bear witness to what is true and dedicate ourselves to living in harmony with it.

We also bear witness in worship to what is broken—the pastoral dimension of the experience of worship. The word "pastor" derives from a Latin word meaning shepherd. According to the Christian New Testament, Jesus once told a parable to some religious leaders who complained that he spent too much time associating with people of ill repute. Jesus responded with a story about a shepherd who was responsible for one hundred sheep, but discovered that one of them had been lost. The shepherd left his ninety-nine sheep in the wilderness and pursued the one that was lost. When he found the sheep, he placed it on his shoulders and rejoiced. Then he went home, called his friends together, and said, "Rejoice with me, for I have found my sheep that was lost" (Luke 15:6).

Sometimes we need to set aside what will result in the greatest good for the greatest number. If one person is in trouble, everyone else must wait. Broken hearts, wounded spirits, failed relationships, shattered dreams: as members of a religious community, we have a place to turn when times get tough. In worship, we bear witness to this aspect of our covenant with each other. We bear witness to what's broken in our lives and our world, and we commit ourselves to help fix it.

We also bear witness in worship to what is right. The Hebrew Bible relates an iconic story about the prophet Elijah, who confronted the people of Israel during a time when many had begun to worship a Phoenician god named Ba'al. "How long will you go limping with two different opinions?" Elijah thundered. If the Lord is God, then follow God; but if Ba'al is God, then follow Ba'al (1 Kings 18:21). The role of the prophet is to delineate the line between what's right and what's not, and to compel people to make a choice.

In this sense, Dr. Martin Luther King Jr. served our nation as an exemplary prophet. He recognized the deep spiritual paradox of a nation founded on a belief in the equality of all yet created by stealing land from Native Americans and built by the labor of slaves from Africa. The American dream was a dream only for some, King pointed out; for others, it had been a nightmare. Dr. King described this central paradox of our nation as the American dilemma: "The hour is late; the clock of destiny is ticking out. It is trite, but urgently true, that if America is to remain a first-class nation she can no longer have any second-class citizens" (pp. 208–209).

Bob Dylan put it this way in one of his songs: "Gotta Serve Somebody." He suggests that the person or purpose you serve may be divine or it may be devilish, but life always advances some overarching intention. Choose this day to pursue a worthy purpose. Choose this day to embody an exemplary virtue. Choose this day to uphold a noble value. In worship, we bear witness to what is right and commit ourselves to serving it.

We also bear witness to what is transcendent—the experience of being connected to everything. When I speak of God, it is usually in this sense: as our most expansive experience of all that is present, as well as all that is past and all that is possible. No matter how dire our circumstances may be, we find hope in knowing that something is possible beyond what is present. The hallmark of the experience of worship is bearing witness to what transcends a particular time and place.

Because it mediates among the necessities of the past, the realities of the present, and the possibilities of the future, the experience of worship can never be a once-and-done event. Rather, worship is an ongoing practice. Émile Durkheim, one of the founders of the field of sociology, established the principle that ritual is what gives people a sense of belonging, a sense of togetherness, a sense of rootedness. He observed that the higher the level of ritual in a particular family or group, the higher their level of solidarity.

This is especially true in the religious domain, where the rituals of worship remind us to recall our commitments, make known our needs, and voice our gratitude. Devout Jews, for example, offer three sets of prayers each day. In its most rigorous form, Christian practice calls for prayers seven times each day, a cycle known as the Daily Office. Islam requires the faithful to pray five times a day. Across the religious spectrum, the most ancient practice, and the most typical today, focuses on morning and evening prayers. Even among Christians who maintain seven offices, the emphasis is on Lauds and Vespers: morning and evening prayers.

The meaning of these times of contemplation and reflection does not depend upon when they occur or how often, nor is the point the specific content. The Daily Office, for example, may include readings, silence, spoken meditation, perhaps a hymn, in addition to praise and commitment. The point of the Daily Office is the ritual of pausing for contemplation. Like the rising and the setting of the sun, the point is the repetition.

In a book titled *Sabbath: Finding Rest, Renewal, and Delight in Our Busy Lives*, Wayne Muller observes that our days are fashioned of cycles and rhythms. Rituals like the Daily Office—liturgical rituals, as they are called—are meant to be repeated. Why? Muller explains: "We are not supposed to do it right the first time, and then be done with it. We are not supposed to do it better each time until we get it perfect.... The perfection is in the repetition.... This is not about progress, it is about circles, cycles, and seasons, about the way time moves, and things we must remember, because with ever-faster turnings of the wheel it can become easier to forget" (pp. 89–90).

What do we most need to repeat? We need constantly to remind ourselves that our lives are not fully our own, that the gift of life comes to us at the largesse of other people and things—both present and past, both living and non-living, both remembered and forgotten. The proper response to this gift is gratitude, which must become a discipline if we ever hope to make it our own.

I had a conversation over lunch one day with an acquaintance who is a Modern Orthodox Jew, which means that he is mostly Orthodox but doesn't look it. To be more precise, Modern Orthodox Jews try to be both modern and Orthodox. Since I grew up in a Conservative Mennonite community, which could aptly be described as Modern Amish, we had a lot in common. He talked about the rituals and responsibilities of Orthodox life and how much he wanted to hand down the tradition to his then-twelve-year-old daughter.

He surprised me by saying that he doesn't pay much attention when the rabbis insist that the Bible is historically accurate. It doesn't matter either way, he said; that's not why I read the Bible. The reason I wear a yarmulke, he added, is not that I think I must or that something bad will happen to me if I don't. The reason I wear it as I go about my business each day is to help me remember who I am and to remind me of commitments I have made.

This is precisely the point of the disciplines of religion: they help us remember who we are and remind us of the commitments we have made. In so doing, they help us transform our lives and our world. Both Jews and Catholics have an exemplary and long standing system of remembrance, as do Muslims: their symbols and sacraments are thick with meaning, and their stories are rife with significance. The music composed over the centuries for daily prayers and communion services in various Christian traditions remains some of the best-loved music in the Western canon. The fact that these particular liturgical forms often bear content that's not relevant to the modern world doesn't mean that similar forms can't and shouldn't be used to bear different content. These forms help us remember who we are and remind us of commitments we have made. Exactly where the reminders came from and how they got to us is almost beside the point. Following the Ten Commandments is a good idea, regardless of whether or not Moses wrote them or even if they came from a divine source. Most of the teachings in the Sermon on the Mount provide wise guidance, regardless of whether or not Jesus actually said them.

If you've rejected the Bible as the one authoritative revelation of the one true God, you still need to establish a rhythm of reflection and reminder for yourself, a means of resetting your moral compass and renewing your moral purpose. At All Souls, for example, we've instituted a daily spiritual practice to focus our spiritual intention and unite us as a religious community even when we're not together. The practice is adapted from a form of focused meditation known in Latin as *lectio divina*, or divine reading.

Originally developed by third-century Christians as a way to read scripture, it was adopted by nineteenth-century Unitarians as a means of spiritual formation. Ralph Waldo Emerson called it "provocative reading"—an approach to reading spiritual texts designed to provoke us into new ways of thinking and living. The practice is quite straightforward: take a short text, read it over several times, and then meditate upon its meaning for your life. You could use W. H. Auden's poem "Leap Before You Look," for example, or Naomi Shihab Nye's poem "Kindness," or Langston Hughes's poem "A Dream Deferred." The purpose is to provoke: you should come away thinking about your life in a slightly different way. You can do this practice anywhere you happen to be, at any time of day, for however long you choose.

The discipline of provocative reading is a personal spiritual practice that can help spark our moral imaginations and set our moral compasses as individuals. But the practice also has a larger religious purpose. Since—ideally at least—everyone within a community of faith will be reading the same short text on the same day, this practice will help ensure unity of purpose. Over time, the themes of daily texts can become interwoven throughout the common life of a religious community. They form part of the common conversation—the family discussion—among people in a religious community on their religious journey.

The definitive statement of a religious tradition's common conversation is usually known as a scripture. The stories, poems, proverbs, and other teachings form an authoritative catalog that defines the self-understanding of a religious community—its distinctive identity and unique purpose. Because religion operates in the realm of transcendent experiences and ultimate aspirations, adherents to a particular tradition can easily succumb to the temptation of believing that their scripture is not only definitive for them, but definitive, period: for all people and all time. This temptation can lead to the sin of scriptural idolatry, the belief that the initial or current form of the scripture remains inviolable.

The reason that religions must evolve and the content of their disciplines must change over time is that the needs people face inevitably change as time passes and history takes shape. The purpose of religion is to enable each of us to unite our deepest needs and highest aspirations with the people around us and everything else, including all that is past and all that is possible. In this way, religion at its best serves the goal of transforming our lives and our world.

In many cases, I don't know the precise nature of the longing or burden people bring with them into the sanctuary at All Souls. I don't know what part of their lives needs to be transformed—what they need to give up or take up, what they need to hold onto more firmly or let go of more fully. I don't know how they have failed themselves or their loved ones during the previous week. I don't know how they have stumbled in their efforts to make their mark at work or school, or to make a difference in the larger community and world. I don't know what persistent worries keep them awake in the night or what thwarted dreams haunt their daylight hours.

But one thing I do know: the common life of a community of faith can be, in the poet Mark Strand's inspired turn of phrase, "a place of constant beginning" (p. 49). In a safe and sacred space, surrounded and supported by a community of faith and all it represents and provides, anyone can begin again.

As the hallmark of a community of faith, worship keeps us in touch with what is true about ourselves and about our world. Worship is also religious practice. It's where we learn how to wait and listen, how to be truthful and faithful. It's where we learn to be present to ourselves, to each other, and to the God holding us all in a divine embrace.

CHAPTER 8

# How We Should Live

## The Source of Ethics

Shall I leave my husband or stay the course? Shall I send my daughter to public school or private school? Shall I start a wholesale flower business or go to seminary? Shall I take the job in Minneapolis or stay in New York?

When people come to my office and ask me about their dilemmas, they're not usually asking me to make decisions for them. Rather, they're asking how they should think about questions like these. How do we make decisions about how we should live?

At its best, religion creates a way of life that enables its adherents to distinguish right from wrong, good from evil, righteous from sinful. Traditional religions feature a set of ethical guidelines from a supernatural God—the Ten Commandments handed down by Moses, for example, or Jesus's Sermon on the Mount. While most of these teachings pass modern muster as guidelines for living, many of the rules and regulations accompanying them (Leviticus in the Hebrew Bible, for example, or 1 Timothy in the Christian New Testament) do not. They advocate ways of life that seem either puzzling (don't wear clothing made of mixed fabrics) or perverse (if a woman's husband dies, marry her off to her dead husband's oldest brother; women should remain silent in church). Where do we look for moral guidance when many religious edicts seem outdated, or irrelevant, or even downright wrong?

Or do we even need moral guidance in the modern world? One of the assumptions underlying the practice of modern statecraft is that people can make their own decisions about how to live if the state ensures that they are free to do so. On these terms, the duty of the state is to ensure that each citizen is maximally free to pursue whatever way of life he or she chooses, consistent with the equal freedom of all other citizens to do the same. In principle, whether you spend your leisure time volunteering in a homeless shelter, tending your vegetable garden, or watching pornography on the Internet makes no difference to the state—unless your overuse of pesticides pollutes your neighbor's water supply or your taste in porn involves sex with minors. The state does use tax policy to encourage certain kinds of behavior, such as buying a home and making donations to your house of worship. The fundamental commitment of the state, however, is to secure the unalienable right of each citizen to, as the US Declaration of Independence puts it, "Life, Liberty, and the pursuit of Happiness"—whatever that may be for each citizen and wherever he or she may find it.

When it comes to the question of how we ought to live, then, does replacing "Do what God says" with "Do whatever you want" count as progress? Yes, but only as a first step. It's like going from "You have to live with your parents" to "You can live anywhere you want." Great—but where do you want to live? The fact that you can live anywhere you want doesn't mean that you don't need to live somewhere in particular, even if that somewhere is under a bridge in a cardboard box. God's not going to tell you how to live. Nor is the government going to tell you which vocation to choose and how to spend your leisure time. You have to figure these matters out for yourself. This doesn't mean that you should ignore everything except the whim of the moment. Rather, you should take everything you know into account as you decide what to do and how to live.

In a secular age, the process of establishing ethical standards is more complicated than opening a book of scripture or doing what seems right in our own minds. This is where I believe enlightened faith enters the picture—faith that views ancient wisdom traditions with appropriate respect but not blind allegiance and gives contemporary sources of knowledge all the trump cards but not the entire deck. Over the centuries, we've discovered the hard way that divine revelation alone won't save us; neither will scientific knowledge alone.

Enlightened religion seeks to unite the best of the wisdom traditions with the best of modern knowledge in order to forge ethical ideas that give our lives meaning and purpose.

Ethical principles set the overall standards we use to make decisions. If the desire to be happy in life conflicts with following the rules, which should we choose? If we choose happiness, should it be our own happiness or the happiness of everyone? If we look for rules to follow, where should we find them and how should we justify them?

Ethical principles also help us negotiate competing interests. Is it right to be dishonest if it serves a good cause? Can we justify living comfortably while people elsewhere in the world are suffering? What obligations do we have to the other creatures with whom we share this planet and to the generations of humans who will come after us? Ethical principles attempt to mediate any conflict we might experience between what we want to do and what we ought to do, between desire and duty.

Ethical principles also help us resolve practical dilemmas. Should we tell a friend that her husband is cheating on her? Should we intervene when we believe an argument between a father and a child is getting too rough? Should we support a politician whose public policies we like but whose personal character we find unattractive? How do we decide these questions?

Sometimes ethical dilemmas involve two competing good options. One Sunday during services, a member of my congregation—an African American woman—told us about a difficult decision her parents once had to make. Her father was a personnel manager in Boston during the mid-1970s, and he was offered the opportunity to become general manager of a television station in Jackson, Mississippi. No black man had ever held that position; in fact, the station was forced by the FCC to put a black management team in place after the former owners had used the station as a tool against black civil rights activists. After weighing the two alternatives, the family decided to move to Jackson.

Their arrival in Mississippi was greeted by the burning of a cross on the lawn of the station. "I was too young to understand what was going on," she said, "but as I matured, I realized that all of this hate was contained in what is the most religious state in the country." When religion turns demonic, how do you weigh confronting evil against keeping your family safe?

Late one night, my phone rang at home. The caller was a member of the congregation and an attorney who worked for an organization that provided publicly funded defenders for people accused of crimes. He faced a dilemma, he explained. The attorneys in his organization had gone out on strike the previous day, and management had responded with an ultimatum: return to work the following morning at 9:00 a.m. or lose your jobs. As a union steward, the caller had been assigned to run one of the picket lines in the morning. In addition to his personal quandary about whether to picket or return to work, he also voiced concern about "the ugly scene that might occur when some of my friends and colleagues tried to cross the line to save their jobs while others, soon to be unemployed, confronted those who crossed over, denounced them as scabs, and ultimately expelled them from what was left of the union." What should he do, he wondered? Where did his ultimate loyalties lie? Fortunately, the union leadership decided a few hours later to return to work, and the crisis passed. But what if it hadn't?

What we need in situations like these is a yardstick we can hold up to the various options to measure which is best. Martha Nussbaum refers to a moment in Plato's *Republic*, when Socrates is discussing the nature of justice with his enthusiastic friends, who have squeezed in a little philosophy between a festival and an evening torch race. But they seem to regard the discussion as a competitive game, not as a serious inquiry. Socrates scolds them. Remember, he says, "It is no chance matter we are discussing, but how one should live" ("Four Paradigms," p. 465).

Ethics and morality are both concerned with proper conduct, but in somewhat different ways. Ethics comes from a Greek word meaning "character," and morality comes from a Latin word meaning "custom" or "habit." In common usage today, morality usually refers to the rules we follow. Ethics is concerned with rules themselves: where they come from and how we justify them. Ethics asks upon what principle we as human beings base our moral rules.

Let's begin with two well-known ethical dilemmas. As with all such puzzles, you must accept the situation as it stands—no fair calling in either Harry Potter or the 101st Airborne. Here's the first dilemma, a version of which was first proposed by Philippa Foot in an *Oxford Review* article in 1967. You are standing alongside a railroad track, near a crossover switch that determines which of two tracks the oncoming train will use. If you do nothing, the approaching train will kill five people who are standing on the track that is currently in use. If you throw the switch, however, the train will cross over to a different track, where only one person is standing and will be killed. You do not know any of the six people. What do you do? Many people, when asked this question, say they would throw the switch.

Here's the second dilemma, a version of which was first proposed by Judith Jarvis Thomson in a *Yale Law Review* article in 1985. You are a physician, and you have five desperately ill people in a hospital unit who need various organ transplants. Unless they receive the transplants very soon, they will die. Just then, a healthy person wanders into the unit. Do you take the organs from the one healthy person, who will thereby die, in order to save the lives of the five? In this case, almost everyone says that they could never do such a thing.

Moral philosophers describe the difference between the two options available to the person at the railroad switch as the difference between doing what is good (saving as many people as possible) and what is right (refraining from killing). However we may describe the difference between these two concepts, we know that good and right mean something. Our ability even to understand the dilemmas of the train and the transplants shows that values such as good and right, and wrong and evil, are part of our experience.

The question is where these values come from. For much of human history, people have looked toward the heavens for a moral matrix. They believed that the God who created the Earth and its people had also given them rules to live by—the Ten Commandments, the laws of Moses, the teachings of Jesus or Mohammed, and so on. Over time, people began to realize that these rules are often inconsistent, even contradictory. They are neither infallible nor, in the strict sense, divine. Rather, they are occasionally inspired human words cloaked in divine garb.

The contemporary philosopher Simon Blackburn likes to tell a story about a high-powered ethics institute that had invited representatives of the major world religions to a forum. Each spoke in turn about the fundamental beliefs of his or her tradition. First, the Buddhist spoke of the path to enlightenment, about the mastery of desire, and the way to achieve inner calm. The panelists all responded, "Wow, terrific, if that works for you, that's great!" Then the Hindu spoke about the cycles of suffering and birth and return, about the teachings of Krishna and the way to release, and they all said, "Wow, terrific, if that works for you, that's great!"

And so on, until the Catholic priest talked of the message of Jesus Christ, the promise of salvation, and the way to life eternal, and they all said, "Wow, terrific, if that works for you, that's great!" Then the priest thumped the table and cried, "No! It is not a question of if it works for me! It's the true word of the living God, and if you don't believe it you're all damned to Hell!" And they all said, "Wow, that's terrific, if that works for you, that's great!" (*Being Good*, p. 26).

If our standards of behavior don't come from a supernatural revelation, this anecdote suggests, perhaps we simply make them up. Different people at different times devise different rules. Perhaps there is no one truth, only different truths embraced by different communities. This situation is commonly known as moral relativism. If relativism is the ultimate ethical principle, however, then tolerance becomes the highest moral virtue. The problem is that some actions are intolerable, no matter who commits them, or when, or where. We need a higher standard than individual preference upon which to establish our code of conduct.

There remains but one final place to look. The third answer is that, in any given situation, we ought to do whatever an *ethical* person would do in that situation—a person who lives as a human being *ought* to live. In other words, look within: within the heart and mind of an ethical person. This approach, while more relevant to the modern world than the other two, also happens to be ancient as well.

Aristotle, in his *Nicomachean Ethics*, suggested a way of addressing this issue that has dominated the discussion ever since. Aristotle believed that both things and people could be judged successful if they achieved their ultimate purpose in life, which is to realize their full potential. The question of potential, in Aristotle's way of thinking, has to do with what is distinctive or unique about something. A knife, for example, has the distinctive ability to cut things, and thus a sharp knife, well used, has achieved a state of virtue.

The distinctive capacity of human beings, Aristotle observed, is the capacity to reason. Our ultimate goal, therefore, is to develop our rational powers and live in accordance with them. In this way, we will achieve the state of virtue that Aristotle calls blessedness or happiness.

The challenge, on these terms, is to develop a standard of conduct that any person who is rational will have no choice but to accept. What might that standard be? In the late eighteenth century, German philosopher Immanuel Kant proposed that rational people must agree to act only on principles that they believe should become universal law. Kant called this requirement the categorical imperative: all people who fit into the category of rational must live this way. To schoolchildren everywhere, this principle shows up when a parent asks, usually in exasperation, "What if everyone acted that way?"

A century later in England, Jeremy Bentham and John Stuart Mill developed a different standard, one that came to be known as utilitarianism. Based on the view that an action is right if it promotes happiness and wrong if it produces the opposite of happiness, they articulated the rule of utility: the good is whatever brings the greatest happiness to the greatest number of people.

While both of these standards have much to commend them, they ultimately seem unwieldy and unsatisfying. It's almost always hard to calculate the greatest good for the greatest number, and the fact that people act in different ways for different reasons often makes the world better, not worse. And sometimes the right thing to do serves the needs of the few and disregards the desires of the many.

Besides—here's the crux of the problem—we as human beings are constituted by more than our rationality. We need an ethical standard that unites our minds and our bodies with everything that makes our experiences possible: the people and the world around us, as well as all that is past and all that is possible.

In my view, the most promising standard emphasizes virtue, which is the disciplined effort to become the best, morally speaking. The English word "virtue" derives from the ancient Latin word *vir*, which means "man." To be virtuous is to be most fully whatever a human being ought to be. Virtue is the discipline whereby we become fully human.

How do we achieve this goal? By developing a discipline of individual moral excellence. In Latin, *virtus* means "manliness" or "valor," especially on the battlefield. For the ancient Greeks, the idea of virtue applied not only to battle, but to every aspect of life. The Greek word *aretē*—usually translated as "virtue" or "excellence"—actually means "being the best you can be" or "reaching your highest human potential." This is not easy to accomplish, however. Even Aristotle concedes that "it is no easy task to be good." Anyone can act: get angry, give money, or speak to friends. But, Aristotle says, to do something "to the right person, and to the right amount, and at the right time, and for the right purpose, and in the right way" is not easy (*Nicomachean Ethics*, 2.9.2).

Even so, in a culture that champions the individual at every turn, an ethic based on virtue seems right. Capitalism, democracy, and Protestantism emerged as the individual became the point of fulcrum in the realms of economics, politics, and religion. Virtue emerges as an ideal when the individual becomes the point of fulcrum in the ethical realm.

The problem, however, is that virtue has fallen out of favor over the centuries since Aristotle. As the Christian tradition developed, it lost its confidence in the human ability to do good. Augustine insisted that humanity had been irreparably damaged by the fall from original perfection, when Adam and Eve disobeyed God in the Garden of Eden. Because of that "original sin," Augustine believed humanity had been enslaved by sin. In other words, virtue became impossible.

Now that we've seen the humanity of the commandments and the fallacy of the fall, I believe it's time for a renaissance of virtue. In a culture that champions the individual, virtue is an approach to ethics that individuals can believe in. And it gives us a way to respond religiously in a world where many people act horribly. Over the past sixty years, the language of human rights has become a vital political tool in our efforts to extend the domain of civilization and the rule of law. And the language of virtue can once again become a vital religious tool in our efforts to extend the domain of morality and the rule of character.

In religious terms, the process of cultivating virtue leads to salvation not by grace or by faith, but to salvation by character. This approach to ethics has been described by the philosopher Richard Taylor as the ethics of aspiration, which emphasizes the kind of people we aspire to become, as opposed to the ethics of duty, which emphasizes rules that have been laid down by someone else (pp. 4–10).

To be sure, there are rules we must follow in life. But even animals can be taught to follow rules. Human beings, in contrast, have the ability to develop character—to fulfill our potential as human beings. Virtuous is to human as pungent is to pepper or sharp is to knife: it's the state of being everything we can possibly be.

Of course, pepper can be pungent without its pungency having any effect, whether it's missing from scrambled eggs or from catfish filets dredged in cornmeal and fried in vegetable oil. And a knife can be sharp without cutting anything or without cutting the right thing. Instead of slicing an heirloom tomato for a sandwich or sharpening a stick for a marshmallow roast, a sharp knife can be used to commit a robbery or deface a mosque. Virtue requires both the ability to act rightly and the knowledge of what constitutes acting rightly.

In the remainder of this chapter, we'll focus on the first of these two challenges: the *ability* to act rightly, which requires us to develop wisdom and courage. In the next chapter, we'll explore how the ethic of gratitude enables us to know *how* we should act when we act rightly.

Wisdom, the dictionary tells us, is the ability to judge rightly in matters of life and conduct. Wisdom requires discernment: not all facts are equally relevant, not all motivations are equally commendable, and not all potential outcomes are equally laudable.

In case you think of wisdom as something that happens under a lotus tree while sipping herbal tea and reciting ancient epigrams, think again. Wisdom is not for the faint of heart. After all, Jesus did not tell his followers to be wise as owls, whatever that means. No, he told them to be wise as serpents—adding, on a more cheerful note, that they should also be innocent as doves, whatever that means (Matthew 10:16).

King Solomon, supposedly the wisest of the ancient Hebrew kings, revealed the cunning side of wisdom. Solomon earned his acclaim as a wise man when, as the story goes, two women came before him to settle a dispute. The women lived in the same house, and they had both recently given birth to sons. In the night, one mother rolled over and accidentally smothered her infant child. Upon awakening to this horrible discovery, she exchanged her dead baby for the living baby of the other mother. In the morning, the other mother discovered the ruse and laid a charge against the first mother, who denied making the exchange.

Solomon's response was decisive, if brutal. He took a sword and said he would cut the living baby in half and give half to each. One of the women became distraught and begged the king to relent, offering to allow the other mother to have the child. Solomon recognized the distraught woman as the living infant's mother and immediately gave the baby to her.

The point of this story is that wisdom requires a deep understanding of human nature. The story also suggests that wisdom emerges when the stakes are high and the consequences are far-reaching. Sometimes, metaphorically at least, wisdom requires a sword—and probably a sharp one at that.

This is not how we're accustomed to thinking of wisdom. Rather, we think of wisdom as a mysterious quality that comes to people who have achieved some level of experience or some measure of enlightenment. When a pediatrician walks into an examining room after a lifetime of seeing children, for example, she can often tell at a glance whether her latest patient is seriously sick or not. She's seen hundreds to thousands of patients each year for forty years, giving her tens of thousands of points of reference. Subtle patterns emerge that she recognizes, allowing her instinctively to make judgments based on subtle differences.

Assertions made by prophets and sages can be equally enigmatic. Like seasoned physicians, however, supposedly wise people can also be wrong. Some of what passes for wisdom isn't. It may sometimes be true that "good things come to those who wait," as the proverb says; or that "the secret of existence is to have no fear," as the Buddha says; or that "the first will be last, and the last will be first," as Jesus says. But at other times, these so-called wise sayings are simply wrong. Sometimes nothing comes to those who wait. Sometimes the first are first, and the last are last.

While wisdom accrues through experience, it develops as a state of mind. Indeed, the original form of the word "wisdom" is the word "wit," which means "mind" or "the faculty of thinking and reasoning." When we say, "I am at my wit's end," we are saying that we're in a situation that has exhausted our ability to think and reason.

The root of wisdom, then, is nothing more—and nothing less—than the ability to keep our wits about us. It's the ability to think clearly in difficult situations—to pay attention to what matters and ignore what doesn't.

Sometime when you won't be traveling by plane for a while, read William Langewiesche's book titled *Fly by Wire: The Geese, the Glide, the Miracle on the Hudson*. It tells the story of US Airways flight 1549, which struck a flock of Canada geese shortly after departing from LaGuardia Airport on January 15, 2009. With both engines disabled, Captain Chesley "Sully" Sullenberger ditched the plane in the Hudson River off midtown Manhattan; all 155 passengers and crew survived.

Langewiesche notes that Captain Sullenberger was a diligent and skilled pilot, but he possessed another attribute that many people overlooked: "He was capable of intense mental focus and exceptional self-control" (p. 9). He was able to pay attention to the right things at the right time.

Langewiesche goes on to explain that these traits normally don't matter much for airline pilots "because teamwork and cockpit routines serve well enough." But Sullenberger's mental focus "emerged in full force during the glide to the Hudson, during which Sullenberger had ruthlessly shed distractions, including his own fear of death" (p. 9). In other words, he kept his wits about him.

The process of keeping our wits about us has two components. One has to do with what's happening in our own minds, and the other concerns what's happening in the minds of the people around us. We need to pay attention to both.

Nearly 2,500 years ago, the Chinese warrior Sun Tzu wrote a book titled *The Art of War*. In one passage, Sun Tzu explains the importance of knowing ourselves and others. He says, "So it is said that if you know others and know yourself, you will not be imperiled in a hundred battles; if you do not know others but know yourself, you win one and lose one; if you do not know others and do not know yourself, you will be imperiled in every single battle" (III.18).

Soldiers are human beings, Sun Tzu says, and they all have loyalties and aversions. You need to know what they will flee from and what they will stand up to, what they will die for and at what cost they will surrender. You need to know what holds them together and what can drive them apart. You need to know the same things about yourself. The ultimate strategy championed by *The Art of War* is to use knowledge of yourself and those around you in order to win without fighting, or if combat is ultimately necessary, to accomplish the most by doing the least.

One of the most serious obstacles to knowing ourselves is what psychologists call "myside bias." As Christopher Peterson and Martin Seligman explain in their reference volume titled *Character Strengths and Virtues*, myside bias refers to our tendency to continue thinking in ways that favor our current views (pp. 144–152). Once we adopt an opinion or reach a conclusion, we tend to seek out evidence that supports our point of view, while ignoring or dismissing evidence to the contrary. Left unchecked, this tendency yields decisions based on selective evidence. This is not the path to wisdom.

The antidote to myside bias is simple to state but hard to put into practice. We need to look for evidence contrary to our current opinions and conclusions, and we need to weigh such evidence fairly when we find it. If you think you are a fine parent to your children or an adequate partner to your spouse, for example, look for evidence that you sometimes fall short. If you think people are poor because they are lazy, look for evidence that you're wrong. In order to keep our wits about us, we need to know ourselves—which includes knowing our biases and watching out for our blind spots.

We also need to know the people around us. Begin with the assumption that other people have different wits than you do, and that even if they say or do the same things as you, they may do so for different reasons. They live in a different world. Figure out what disappoints them and what gives them hope. Assess their motives and judge their actions. Sometimes wisdom requires us to be intolerant. We need to know the people around us: what commitments they have made and which paths they are on.

If we keep our wits about us, we'll make good decisions in the short run. We'll also develop the kind of deep insight and accrue the kind of broad experience that counts for wisdom over the long run. Solomon became Solomon by keeping his wits about him. We can do the same. We can learn to know ourselves and learn to know the people around us. We can be honest with ourselves and set the same standard for others. Then, when we need to decide which of the paths before us leads to virtue, we'll have the wisdom to know the difference between a bad option and a good option or, what is more likely, between a good option and a slightly better one or a bad option and a slightly less-bad option.

But once we decide what to do, we also need the confidence to act. One of Plato's many dialogues tells the story of a conversation among Socrates and two eminent Greek generals, Laches and Nikias. The generals have just watched an exhibition by soldiers who are fighting in armor, a new form of combat. In the future, Laches and Nikias wonder, will the best education include learning this new skill? Socrates uses the occasion to explore what it means to be courageous.

When asked by Socrates to say what courage is, Laches replies, that's easy enough. Anyone who stays at his post, faces the enemy, and doesn't run away, you may be sure is courageous.

Surely courage is more than staying put in battle, Socrates replies. Sometimes great victories are won by falling back and regrouping. Besides, people can be courageous in other areas of life: against the perils of the sea, for example, or against disease or poverty. People can also be courageous in public affairs or in facing their own desires and pleasures.

This is quite true, Laches agrees.

So, Socrates continues, what is this thing, courage, which is the same in all of these cases?

Perhaps courage is a certain endurance of the soul, Laches ventures.

But what if someone endures in doing something that is foolish, or hurtful, or mischievous, Socrates replies. Is that courage?

Obviously not, Laches admits.

At this point Socrates mercifully turns to Nikias, who tries a different approach. Nikias ventures that courage is somehow related to the goal being sought or the danger being avoided. He eventually concludes that courage requires wisdom—the knowledge of what is good and worthy of being pursued, as well as what is evil and must therefore be avoided. As Socrates puts it, summarizing Nikias's argument, "Courage is knowledge not merely of what is to be dreaded and what dared, but practically a knowledge concerning all goods and evils at every stage" (199D).

The essence of courage, in other words, is not merely the ability to do something that is physically risky. You demonstrate courage when you know what is worthy and are willing to pursue it, no matter if the road is long and the path unclear. You also demonstrate courage when you know what is wrong and are willing to confront it, no matter if the risk is great and the outcome uncertain.

In other words, you cannot demonstrate courage merely by plunging down a black diamond ski trail at breakneck speed, although courage sometimes requires facing significant risks. Nor can you demonstrate courage merely by leaping out of a plane with a parachute, although courage always requires grappling with fear. Rather, courage is the ability to do two things. It is the ability see good in the distance and take a step toward it—despite obvious risks. It is also the ability to see evil close at hand and take steps to confront it—despite present danger. To know courage is to know a calling that is greater than fear.

The English word "courage" derives from a French word that means "heart." This is a useful etymology. The work of the heart is not to pump a vast amount of blood in an instant and then rest for a season. Rather, the heart works best when its rhythm adapts to the needs of the moment.

Courage is like that, too. There is a cadence to courage: a responsive rhythm of achieving what is good and confronting what is not. Courage does not eliminate fear; it sees a path through the fear to the calling that lies beyond. The key to courage is not the fear but the calling.

Theodore Olson responded to a calling greater than fear when he wrote the cover article for *Newsweek* magazine's January 8, 2010, issue titled "The Conservative Case for Gay Marriage." Best known as the Republican lawyer who won the case of *Bush v. Gore* in 2000, Olson wrote the article to try to help overthrow Proposition 8 in California, which in effect banned same-sex marriage. In the article, he argued that the constitution requires extending the benefits of marriage to same-sex partners and that conservatives and liberals alike should actively support the legalization of same-sex marriage.

Olson's decision to champion same-sex marriage illustrated his ability to see good in the distance and take a step toward it—despite obvious risks to his standing as a conservative. After he took up this cause, Olson said he was subjected to anger, resentment, and hostility, as well as to words like "betrayal." But he was also overwhelmed by expressions of gratitude and goodwill. He said, "I have been particularly moved by…how lonely and personally destructive it is to be treated as an outcast and how meaningful it will be to be respected by our laws and civil institutions as an American, entitled to equality and dignity." He added, "I have no doubt that we are on the right side of this battle, the right side of the law, and the right side of history." To know courage is to know a calling that is greater than fear.

Several years ago, I received an e-mail from a longtime member of All Souls. She had worked successfully in the media world for a couple of decades, but had also begun teaching yoga classes on the side. Over time, she developed a desire to teach yoga and meditation full time—and thought she had a plan for making the move. Then the economic crisis struck in 2008.

She wrote, "As were so many other members of the media world, I was very hard hit this past year-and-a-half by the economic downturn. The stock option shares I was so prudently managing—and that were intended to fund the next three years of transitioning into the much lower pay scale of a yoga and meditation teacher—disappeared one particularly tumultuous afternoon. After a short period, spent mostly sitting in my living room in a complete panic, I decided to do what in retrospect was quite uncharacteristic for me: I took the less safe route. I decided to go with my gut and follow the path I'd started down, knowing that it would mean continued economic challenge."

She reported that so far things were going well. She found deep satisfaction in her work. She teaches yoga to HIV/AIDS patients in the South Bronx and to people who suffer from arthritis. She embarked on a two-year yoga therapist training program. Reflecting on the financial crisis that impelled her decision, she said that while "the exercise in massive non-attachment was not particularly welcome, it helped me to walk my talk and realize that the most important thing is truly the most important thing." To know courage is to know a calling that is greater than fear.

Courage is the ability see good in the distance and take a step toward it—despite obvious risks. It is also the ability to see evil close at hand and take steps to confront it—despite present danger. In their book *Half the Sky: Turning Oppression into Opportunity for Women Worldwide*, Nicholas Kristof and Cheryl WuDunn tell the story of Mukhtar Mai (pp. 70–79), a story detailed by the playwright Susan Yankowitz in the play *SEVEN*, based on interviews with Mukhtar.

Mukhtar was a teenage peasant girl in a small village in Pakistan when her twelve-year-old brother was falsely accused of having had sex with the daughter of one of the landowners in the village. In retribution, the chief of the landowner clan ordered four of his henchman to gang rape Mukhtar. So they did, taking turns for more than an hour on the floor of a stable, while other men with shotguns forced her father and brother to wait outside. Mukhtar recounts, "When the men are finished with me, I am thrown outside. My clothes are torn and I am nearly naked. I lie on the ground, along with my shame....I will never be the same (*SEVEN*, p. 121).

For several days afterward, no one spoke to Mukhtar about what happened, and she spoke to no one. In Pakistan, Mukhtar explained, women do not talk about such degrading things with others. Some women stay home and never mention it again. Others kill themselves. "Is that what I should do?" Mukhtar wondered. "In Pakistan, staying alive is seen as more cowardly and shameful than the rape itself.... But if I didn't die, what would I do with my life?" (pp. 121–122).

Mukhtar soon learned that her rape was not just a plot of the landowners; it had been ordered by the town council as a so-called honor revenge. Outrageously, such "honor" rapes and killings are all too common in Pakistan. Hundreds of Pakistani women die each year from "honor" killings, almost all at the hands of family members.

The inspiring part of Mukhtar's story is that two people—two men—unexpectedly met Mukhtar's courage with their own and came to her aid: the local imam and the local judge. In one of his Friday sermons, the imam told his congregation that the village council sinned in ordering this violation of Islamic law. The criminals responsible for the rape must be brought to justice. Mukhtar Mai and her family should go to the police and file charges immediately, he said (p. 123).

Mukhtar had never heard of the constitution. She didn't realize that women had legal rights. Even so, her father and brothers went with her to file charges, and she ended up before a judge. He asked her to describe every detail of what happened in the stable. So she did, as the judge bore witness to the travesty of her suffering and gave voice to her cry for help. Before she left the courtroom, the judge told Mukhtar to hold fast to her courage. He knew how explosive her testimony would be (p. 124).

Almost overnight, a commonplace rape involving a voiceless peasant girl in a nameless village became a national scandal in Pakistan and an international outrage around the world. Today, Mukhtar uses money she received from the judgment against her rapists to fund the operation of a school and a clinic in her village.

In Mukhtar's case, it took the courage of three people to stand against evil: a rape victim who decided not to give up, an imam who decided to speak out, and a judge who decided to listen. The key to doing what's right is to focus not on the fear but on the calling.

The question is where that calling comes from. Once we've committed ourselves to being the best, morally speaking, and we've learned to keep our wits about us, and we've screwed our courage to the sticking point, then what? How do we decide what we ought to do in a particular situation? What values do we use to set our moral compasses and from where do those values come? To answer these questions, we turn to the ethics of gratitude.

## CHAPTER 9

# What We Owe

## *An Ethic of Gratitude*

When we ask how we should live, the answer is simple: live the way a human being ought to live. A knife should be sharp; it ought to cut things that need cutting and not cut things that don't. The same principle applies to us as human beings: we should do what humans ought to do and not do what we shouldn't.

Even if you agree with this principle, however, you doubtless wonder what exactly it means. From where does the "should" come? What ought we do? And what does gratitude have to do with it?

My guess is that you haven't often seen the words "ethic" and "gratitude" in the same sentence, much less connected by the word "of." Most people think of gratitude as an expression of appreciation: saying "thank you" if someone holds the door open when you have an armful of groceries or invites you to dinner on Friday evening. How can we possibly develop a rigorous approach to ethics based on a winsome social convention? I agree that an ethic of gratitude sounds counterintuitive at first, even if intriguing, but I'm convinced that it's the best way to think about how we ought to live. My goal in this chapter is to convince you as well.

First, let's look at the alternatives. The religions of the book—Judaism, Christianity, and Islam—base their approach to ethics on a supposedly authoritative revelation from an allegedly supernatural God. In order to live an ethical life, you should obey the commandments of God, or accept salvation from God, or submit to the will of God. In the Christian tradition, the ethical imperative to love God and love your neighbor emerges as the necessary human response to God's creative and redeeming love of humanity.

The fourth-century theologian Augustine believed that love provided sufficient guidance for living. Augustine famously said that if you love God truly, you'll live rightly: you'll become the kind of person you ought to become. But the idea that "love is all you need," as the Beatles would put the same sentiment many centuries later, falls short when we need to decide how to live. For example, the imperative to love your neighbor can, and does, provide theological justification for both the commitment to pacifism and the commitment to just war doctrine. In the name of love, you can "turn the other cheek" or you can take out "an eye for an eye," which nowadays means sending in the drones or launching the cruise missiles.

Besides, the God who "so loved the world, that He gave His only begotten Son" to die on the cross is the same God who created a universe in which people who don't follow his rules eventually burn forever in hell. Some strands of the tradition—especially Presbyterians and others who take their cues from the influential Reformation-era theologian John Calvin—insist that God damned the hell-bound people to hell before he even created the world. No matter how you define love, this preemptive damnation doesn't seem to be an exemplary instance of love—and certainly not of love at its best.

I'm not arguing that love isn't, as Shakespeare once said, "a many-splendored thing." The word "love" has as many meanings in English as the Inuits have words for snow. I tell my wife I love her at the end of every day, I tell my congregation I love them at the end of every sermon, and I declare that I love pecan pie at the end of every slice, if not every bite. Each of these invocations of love, all heartfelt, carries a different meaning. But no one meaning of love alone, nor all possible meanings of love put together, provide a reasonable and practical basis for making tough decisions about how to live.

For an ethical imperative to have relevance in the modern world, it needs to be more like the law of gravity than the Ten Commandments: grounded in the nature of things, not in a supposedly divine set of commands developed three thousand years ago. The point of fulcrum for an ethic of gratitude is not revelation but agency. Ethics becomes relevant at the point where the capacity to decide and the ability to act are present. That point, it turns out, occurs initially in the human realm and only subsequently shows up in the divine realm. For this reason, an ethic of gratitude takes human agency with ultimate seriousness.

As we discussed in chapter two, everything that exists owes its existence to a complex set of relationships that—if you trace the relationships all the way out through space and all the way back in time—ultimately involves everything. As humans, for example, we are utterly dependent upon the parents who conceived us, the plants and animals that daily provide our nourishment, the trees that give us oxygen, the sun that warms the atmosphere, and so on—out through space and back in time. We are constituted by these relationships. This principle applies to everything whatsoever. Nothing is what it is strictly within itself.

Two consequences follow from this principle. First, everything that exists is determined, in part, by the relationships that constitute its immediate past. I am who I am by virtue of the experiences I have had. These experiences cannot be changed, as much as I sometimes wish otherwise. My immediate past comes into my present experience with the force of necessity.

Second, nothing can wholly determine the existence of something else. More to the point, no person can wholly determine the being of another person. Even in situations of extreme oppression and coercion, no one can fully determine what another person will think or how they will respond. Because the future has not yet been fully determined, freedom is a strictly universal principle. The future comes into my present experience as the face of possibility.

Given the fact that I have the past that I have (the presence of necessity), I still have some measure of choice, even if it happens to be extremely limited, about how I act or don't act in the future (the presence of possibility). This is why human agency, rather than divine revelation, comes to the fore when thinking about ethics. If you want to know the truth about what experiences I have with me in the present and how I might use those experiences to create the future, look to my decisions—not to divine decrees or blind fate or brute necessity or any other external explanation. In human terms, human agency is the point of fulcrum where necessity meets possibility and the past becomes the future.

Given the pivotal role that human agency plays in this creative advance, we need to ask how we should make decisions. Here's the basic principle: always maximize the value of your present experience for the sake of the future. We'll get to the question of value in a moment. But in the meantime, the point is that experience advances cumulatively: a better past provides better possibilities to emerge for the present. If acted upon, these better possibilities become a more valuable experience in the present, which in turn provides better possibilities for an even more valuable future. Taken as a whole, these experiences— all that is present, as well as all that is past and all that is possible— ultimately find their union in the divine. Whitehead writes:

> *The religious insight is the grasp of this truth: That the order of the world, the depth of reality of the world, the value of the world in its whole and in its parts, the beauty of the world, the zest of life, and the mastery of evil, are all bound together—not accidentally, but by reason of this truth: that the universe exhibits a creativity with infinite freedom, and a realm of forms with infinite possibilities; but that this creativity and these forms are together impotent to achieve actuality apart from the completed ideal harmony, which is God.* (Religion in the Making, *p. 115)*

For Whitehead, the absolute moral principle can be stated simply: cooperate with the creative advance toward ideal harmony. We promote the creative advance when we make choices that increase the complexity and maximize the reciprocity of experience. As we shall see, value is a function of complexity, and freedom is a function of reciprocity.

Let's examine why an increase in complexity increases the value of experience, as well as why a rejection of complexity has the opposite effect. The reason a piano is more musically valuable than a kazoo is that a piano can sound eighty-eight notes, while a kazoo can sound only one noise, and an annoying one at that. On a piano, you can play a Chopin nocturne, or a Rachmaninoff concerto, or Elton John's "Goodbye Yellow Brick Road." On a kazoo, you can't play anything; you can just keep making the same annoying noise.

Again, the reason a backhoe is a more valuable tool than a sharp stick is that a backhoe can perform many different tasks—digging, filling, grading, carrying, and so on—in many different ways, each precisely calibrated (assuming a skilled operator) to the task at hand. With a sharp stick, you can either poke things or not poke things.

In general, value increases as complexity increases because exponentially more options become possible, whether you are trying to make music or create a garden. On these terms, a child whose only choices for how to spend the day are collecting sticks for fire or walking miles for water experiences less value than a child who could collect wood for a barbeque, take a swim in the lake, play in the park, or help a grandparent clean out the garage. This is not to say that the child with fewer options has less value as a person. In fact, the child with fewer options may be more diligent, more courageous, and more selfless that the child with more options. But if our goal is to maximize the present for the sake of the future, having a lot of good options in the present enables us to create more value than having a few poor options.

This principle also works in the other direction. If it's good to create value and maximize possibilities, it's bad to do the opposite—to degrade value and diminish complexity. On these terms, the genocide in Bosnia in 1993 was an effort by the Serbs to reduce a culture that had been ethnically and religiously diverse, and magnificently so—a cultural symphony, one could say—to a cruelly monochrome one: a cultural kazoo, or perhaps the flat-line death sound of a cardiac monitor.

In the summer of 1993, when my daughter Zoë was about four months old, we spent a month visiting her grandparents in England. Buckden, a picture-perfect village just outside Cambridge, featured thatch-roofed cottages, postmen on bicycles, and the workshop of England's sole remaining producer of handmade cricket bats. It was a wonderful place to spend a month.

I often walked with Zoë down the main street of the village early in the morning. Actually, I walked and she rode in her stroller; she preferred it that way. We went to the news agent and bought a copy of the newspaper, then continued on to a bench just opposite the ancient and ivy-covered Buckden Towers. I read the headlines aloud to Zoë, and she gurgled in response, her voice adding a certain perspective to what I read.

One day, I came across a front-page story written by someone who had just escaped from Sarajevo, where the Serbs were engaged in what turned out to be a systematic ethnic cleansing against the Muslims and Croats. By the time the genocide ended, more than 8,000 Muslims and Croats would be dead. When I came to the passage about a village full of women and children, a group of Serbian soldiers, and their chain saw, I didn't tell Zoë about that part. In fact, I abruptly stopped reading.

Here's the cruel irony: by most estimates, Bosnia had as good a chance as any place on earth of harvesting the first fruits of diversity. Novelist Dževad Karahasan, a native of Sarajevo who fled to Austria, said the goal of unifying the diverse peoples of Europe had already been achieved by the people of Sarajevo five hundred years ago. Sarajevo appeared to be the prototype of a united Europe.

Karahasan's own background illustrates his point. He was born into a Muslim family, received his education from Franciscan monks, and married a Serb. In the city of Sarajevo itself, he wrote in the *Guardian* newspaper, Jewish, Orthodox, Catholic, and Muslim people have lived and worked side by side for centuries. "In my block of flats," Karahasan pointed out, "there are ten families, only one of which is of purely one nationality." The rate of interracial marriage before the war was about 75 percent.

Then Bosnia became what its Nobel Prize–winning writer Ivo Andrić called a "land of hatred." In his article, Karahasan observed that the people who tried to destroy Sarajevo and obliterate the Muslims were motivated by only one thing: fear—fear of the very diversity that for centuries was the genius of Bosnia. Karahasan wrote, "The foundation of their culture is a one-stringed musical instrument called a *guzla*. The worldview of someone brought up on a one-stringed instrument is confused by a complex structure like my city. It scares them." He concludes, "They are attempting to destroy their own fear. That does not worry me so much as the fact that, in attempting to kill their own fear, they are killing so many children."

I've been told that it's not all that hard to play a one-stringed instrument. My guess is that it's dead easy to play it badly. To play a piano concerto with a symphony orchestra, in contrast, takes skill, dedication, and cooperation. Of course, you can just bang on a piano, which is why value also requires order—a well-ordered complexity. The complexity of an exquisite symphony or a deep friendship or a true community helps us understand how value gets created in our world. An ethic of gratitude envisions a world where everyone has the opportunity to create value—for themselves, as well as for everyone and everything else.

In addition to increasing the complexity of experience, our ethical imperative is also to maximize the reciprocity of experience. Just as value is a function of complexity, freedom is a function of reciprocity. This is a point on which it's easy to become confused, especially in the present-day United States, where the wolf-cry of freedom confronts every suggestion that we as citizens owe anything to either our fellow citizens or the shared sets of intentions and actions we call our government. This state-of-nature point of view—every person pursuing his or her own interests alone—is both descriptively wrong and theologically demonic.

In fact, we owe everything to the people and the world around us. My freedom to flip on the light switch, open the faucet, turn on the television, pour a bowl of cereal, unlock the door, drive to work, deposit my paycheck, make a phone call, check a website, get a physical—the list could go on forever—is strictly contingent. I cannot do any of these things, or at least nothing will happen if I do, unless a lot of other people have done a lot of things upstream, including make laws and establish regulations. In this sense, my freedom increases only as the people and world around me expand my ability to choose and act. Freedom is a function not of independence but of reciprocity. Our freedom to create more value in our own lives depends, ultimately, upon our commitment to use our agency to create a world that contains more value for everyone else as well. As Albert Camus once observed, "Freedom is not made up principally of privileges; it is made up especially of duties" (*Resistance, Rebellion, and Death*, p. 96).

The truth is that we are utterly dependent for everything, even life itself, upon sources beyond ourselves and even beyond our control. I contend that the appropriate religious response to this foundational reality is gratitude. Gratitude becomes an ethic when we respond to this awareness by using our freedom as moral agents to nurture the world that nurtures us in return. An ethic of gratitude demands that we take everything personally because, in order to be a person, we take everything we need from the people and the world around us.

Here's the short version: take everything personally because you personally take everything. We become the kind of people we ought to become when we help create a world that gives us the freedom to create value for ourselves and others—and gives others the freedom to do the same for us.

What does this world look like? It's an orderly world where people have the freedom to make good choices. They have good options from which to choose, and they take personally their obligation to create the kind of world they take personally. These good options and subsequent good choices make the world more valuable and, in turn, enable even more freedom to make even better choices in the future. In ideal terms, Whitehead speaks of "creativity with infinite freedom" and a universe with "infinite possibilities." The goal is for the creative advance to achieve a "completed ideal harmony"—a world that is infinitely valuable and thus infinitely beautiful (*Religion in the Making*, p. 115).

The experience of beauty opens a window onto this ideal vision of life. What makes something or someone beautiful? In her book *On Beauty and Being Just*, Elaine Scarry contends that the attribute most consistently singled out over the centuries to define beauty has been symmetry: a sense of balance and proportion (pp. 91, 96). She rightly points out that we hear those qualities in great music—Bach is a ready example—and we see them in beautiful paintings and beautiful buildings, as well as in beautiful faces and figures. If we're paying attention, she says, a glimpse of the ideal should elicit in us a profound dissatisfaction with experiences that fall short. At its best, beauty confronts and confounds us, directing our attention toward what is absent in our world: symmetry, proportion, balance, equality, justice (pp. 108–109).

The painter Henri Matisse said repeatedly throughout his life that he wanted his paintings to be so beautiful that when one came upon them, all problems would subside (Scarry, p. 33). At its most powerful, beauty both transfixes and transforms us. To be swept away by the aspiration of a Bach oratorio is to become tirelessly impatient with a world where so many children have so little hope. To be stopped short by the simple calm of a Courbet landscape is to recognize that violence has no place in human relations. To be captivated by the elegant symmetry of a Georgian sanctuary is to know the obscene calamity that hunger and poverty represent. To be riveted by the sight of an exuberantly colored butterfly is to know that we must stand strong against those who would crush the fragile and oppress the weak.

Once in a while, in the midst of the chaos and clamor of our lives, we experience something that points us toward a standard or an ideal. It sets a benchmark by which we can measure our conduct and our lives. The experience of beauty gives us a hint of what is possible. Because you are free to take personally all the beauty in the world, you are also obligated to take personally all its ugliness.

As Scarry puts it, the experience of beauty has built-in consequences. The consequences are best captured in our language by a single word, fairness, which refers to both the loveliness of a face and the ethical requirement to be fair, play fair, or distribute fairly. Beauty issues a call to those who encounter it; it creates a covenant with those who experience it. It is a call to symmetry and equality—not just in our music and art, but also in our relations with each other and with our world. Beauty is a call to be just.

John Rawls, an American political philosopher whose thinking about justice has set the terms of the debate for the past several decades, forged an understanding of justice on precisely these terms: justice as fairness, he called it. Rawls published a watershed book in 1971 titled *A Theory of Justice*. Simply put, his approach to justice is a variant of the scenario involving two children, one piece of cake, and the problem of how to divide the cake between the two in an equitable manner. The solution is quite simple: one child cuts the cake into two pieces, while the other has first choice of which piece to eat. Since the child with the knife does not know which piece of cake he will end up with, he has maximum motivation to ensure that both pieces are as big as possible. This will happen only if the two pieces are the same size.

Using the same basic approach in a rather more sophisticated way, Rawls sets out his theory of justice, which he calls justice as fairness (summary on pp. 11–19). As a moral language game, it is designed to include everyone—at least everyone who considers him- or herself rational. In his early writings, Rawls claims that certain moral beliefs are required by the structure of human reason. These beliefs are universal in the conscience of all people and can serve as the foundation of morality. In other words, if you can think, then you have no choice but to agree with the ideas that underlie justice as fairness.

What are those ideas? Rawls imagines a group of people who gather in what he calls the original position, behind a veil of ignorance. The position is original in the "in the beginning" sense, and the veil of ignorance keeps those who choose the principles of justice from knowing certain information. If you and I were in the original position, we would not know exactly who we were in the society, what position we held, or to which generation we belonged. Nor would we have any specific knowledge of our life's goals and plans.

If we were in this original position, behind a veil of ignorance, what would we choose as principles of justice? First, according to Rawls, we would declare a principle of equal liberty: each person is entitled to the greatest total amount of basic liberty, consistent with an equal amount for everyone else. The second principle, which Rawls refers to as the difference principle, would state that any social and economic inequalities must be distributed to the greatest advantage of the least-well-off person. Rawls argues that people in the original position would choose this principle because they would follow what he calls the "maximin" rule: always maximize the minimum possibility. Or, in the less elegant terms we used earlier: if I do not know beforehand which piece of cake I will end up with, then I will do my best to divide the cake fairly.

If you and I were forced to design principles of justice for our nation or (perhaps more tellingly) our world, and if we had no idea what place we would subsequently occupy in either, my guess is that we would do our best to upgrade the downside. I can do the math. The current odds of any randomly chosen person in human history enjoying the level of comfort and well-being that I do now are at least a million—maybe ten million—to one against. If we can think rightly, Rawls insists, we must at times choose and act and legislate as though we are ignorant of our own good fortune. Reason demands it, and justice requires it. Besides, the world is our world; an ethic of gratitude demands that we take it personally.

The ongoing debate in the United States about immigration provides a good test case for Rawls's approach. The question is how we should treat those who are here illegally and how many more immigrants we should permit to enter in the future, and for what reasons. As Aristide Zolberg notes in his book titled *A Nation by Design: Immigration Policy in the Fashioning of America*, the question eventually comes down to how far our obligations as human beings extend. Our obligations certainly extend beyond those we consider our fellow citizens, but how much further? Our citizenship of the world must be tempered by realism. If everyone who wished to come to America were free to do so, there would soon be nothing left worth coming to.

On the other hand, if the pendulum swings too far in the direction of nationalism, the United States and other affluent democracies would need to transform themselves, according to Zolberg, into "police states, protected by a new iron curtain or a Berlin wall" (p. 451). Given our history as a nation of immigrants, he concludes, the burden of proof is on those who want to close the borders. And for those who would keep the borders open, he says, "priority must be given to those in greatest need, people who cannot survive in their country of origin because they are the target of persecution, because of life-threatening violence, or because there is no possible way of making a living" (pp. 456–457).

When it comes to immigration, our nation has a chilling history of sometimes turning the difference principle on its head. In an article about lessons from the Holocaust titled "The Physician-scientist, the State, and the Oath: Thoughts for Our Time" in *The Journal of Clinical Investigation*, Dr. Barry Coller of Rockefeller University in Manhattan describes the history behind the Immigration Act of 1924. At the turn of the twentieth century, the American eugenics movement was in full sway, based on what was considered cutting-edge scientific knowledge from Darwin's theory of evolution and Mendel's discoveries in genetics. The movement's goal was to improve the human race through intentional genetic selection, an effort that received wide support from both the scientific and philanthropic communities.

To some, the next logical step was "to limit the reproductive potential of those judged to be eugenically inferior." In the wake of an Indiana law enacted in 1907, followed by similar laws enacted in twenty-eight other states, including New York, some sixty thousand Americans were sterilized, virtually all with limited or no informed consent. "The Nazis, including Hitler himself, professed great admiration for the American eugenics movement and modeled their own sterilization laws and program on those in the United States" (p. 2568).

Not surprisingly, the Immigration Act of 1924 contained provisions for eugenic screening. It also set immigration quotas "specifically designed to limit immigration of individuals from Eastern Europe because they were judged to be eugenically inferior." This law, Coller concludes, "doomed thousands of Eastern Europeans trying to flee Nazi persecution by denying them the ability to emigrate to the United States" (p. 2568).

We need to remember this shameful history. We also need to remember the Mother of Exiles—the Statue of Liberty—who stands near Ellis Island in New York Harbor. "Give me your tired, your poor," the inscription by Emma Lazarus on her base says, "your huddled masses yearning to breathe free." The difference principle does not tell us specifically where to set immigration limits or how to deal with people who have flouted the law. But it does give us a way to think about our identity as a nation and our responsibility as free people. Those who are least well off and those who are most in need come first.

What would Rawls say about the immigration debate? He would say that changes in immigration policy should not diminish either the economic or the legal prospects of immigrants who are already here illegally. Rawls would also say that policy changes should not reduce the existing chance of success for foreign citizens seeking political asylum or economic refuge in the United States. Another way to solve the problem, of course, is for the United States aggressively to help other nations improve the prospects of their own citizens, thereby reducing the economic and political disparities that motivate people to come here in the first place. The difference principle can work in both directions.

Rawls's conception of justice as fairness, and especially his articulation of the principle of equal liberty and the difference principle, can help us focus our ethic of gratitude. Of course, the ethic of gratitude won't tell us exactly what to do in a particular situation, but it does give us a way to think about our specific responsibilities as human beings. Located at the point of fulcrum where necessity meets possibility and the past becomes the future, an ethic of gratitude insists that we make choices that maximize not only our own freedom to make even better choices in the future, but also the freedom of everyone else to do the same. And we should pay the most attention to situations within our own lives and our world where freedom is scarce and choices are sparse. We should take everything personally, but we should take most personally those situations where agency yields the least.

In fact, most human suffering would disappear if people used their freedom to make worthy choices rather than wicked ones. Martha Nussbaum, in her book *The Fragility of Goodness*, shows how the ancient Greeks distinguished suffering caused by natural forces from suffering caused by divine or human intention. Using the Greek tragic poets as her muse, Nussbaum notes that certain aspects of human life put us at risk and make us vulnerable to suffering (pp. xxix–xxxvii). Ironically enough, the risks come as the shadow side of the very experiences that make life good, such as love, friendship, communal loyalty, and political purpose. Though some forms of human suffering are a necessary counterpoint to our pursuit of the good things in life, most are not.

When we love our children or our partners or our friends, for example, we necessarily risk losing them or otherwise suffering grief as a result of our relationships. Our bodies make it possible for us to experience many things we consider good, from various forms of physical pleasure, to intellectual mastery, to vocational success. Our bodies also make us vulnerable to hunger, disease, and physical assault, but these are neither good nor, in most cases, necessary. The fact that such a high percentage of women suffer from sexual assault is the result of wickedness, not necessity. All humans must die sometime, but the fact that so many die so very young, from either war or preventable illness or hunger, is not at all necessary. Citizenship in a just political system is a good thing, even when our favored policy or candidate loses out. Being imprisoned or tortured or executed by an unjust regime, however, is not a necessary consequence of political engagement.

The question to ask when people suffer is whether the disaster is caused by some necessary element of life or by bad behavior. The answer, Nussbaum insists, is that most human suffering throughout history has been caused by greed, malice, and various other forms of human wickedness. The fact that we require certain things from the world around us in order to live a good life does not give other people the right to make us suffer by taking advantage of our vulnerability. The fragility of human goodness, in other words, stems mainly from the fact that, in Nussbaum's words, "most human beings are lazy or self-preoccupied (or, we might add, racist or nationalist, or in other ways hate-filled, blind to the full humanity of others)" (p. xxxi). The suffering that results from these factors should not count as necessary suffering, but rather as culpable wrongdoing.

When it comes to those who suffer most and whose agency yields least, the situation is this: relatively little of the suffering people experience is necessary. Hunger: not necessary. Starvation: not necessary. Debilitating poverty: not necessary. Genocide: not necessary. Death from preventable diseases: not necessary. Most of the human misery we witness today is the result of either culpable wrongdoing or culpable negligence. People who could help but sit idly by cannot escape responsibility. On the other hand, people who help have done something morally commendable.

An ethic of gratitude insists that we take everything personally. And we should pay the most attention to situations where the malevolent use of human agency has done the most damage. Take everything personally, but take most personally those places where order, value, and beauty are most at risk. After all, the world constitutes your own experience. It's not only your world; it's you.

In many cases, of course, we exercise our agency more through the institutions we sustain—including our religions—than through discrete personal decisions. With some notable exceptions on the lunatic fringe, you don't hear people in the United States today using religion to argue that people of color are inferior to white people. In fact, many of the most effective advocates for racial equality over the past couple of centuries have grounded their prophetic claims in religious faith, an approach that reached its apotheosis in James Cone's declaration in his 1975 book *God of the Oppressed* that "Jesus is Black." Nonetheless, many of our institutions were built and many of our patterns of life developed during times when people believed in white superiority and advanced white privilege. As a result, white people in the United States today possess unearned advantages that most people of color do not.

In his book *How Racism Takes Place*, George Lipsitz says, "It is not so much that Blacks are disadvantaged, but rather that they are taken advantage of by discrimination in employment, education, and housing, by the ways in which the health care system, the criminal justice system, and the banking system skew opportunities and life chances along racial lines" (p. 2). Some of these "collective, cumulative, and continuing forms of discrimination" have specific historical roots. Lipsitz cites the Homestead Act of 1862, which gave away valuable acres of land for free to white families, but expressly precluded participation by blacks. At least 46 million white adults today can trace the origins of their family wealth to that act. The 1934 National Housing Act added equity to the estates of some 35 million white families between 1934 and 1978 while systematically excluding black families. These financial advantages and the lack thereof continue to be passed down the generations.

Lipsitz's main emphasis in the book, however, concerns what he calls "the fatal couplings of place and race in our society." He says:

> *Relations between races are relations between places, as the geographer Laura Pulido demonstrates. White identity in the United States is place bound. It exists and persists because segregated neighborhoods and segregated schools are nodes in a network of practices that skew opportunities and life chances along racial lines. Because of practices that racialize space and spatialize race, whiteness is learned and legitimated, perceived as natural, necessary, and inevitable. Racialized space gives whites privileged access to opportunities for social inclusion and upward mobility. At the same time, it imposes unfair and unjust forms of exploitation and exclusion on aggrieved communities of color. (p. 86)*

For example, a girl born a mile north of where my family and I live in Manhattan would probably end up at a public school in her neighborhood—among the poorest neighborhoods in New York City.

She probably wouldn't end up at P.S. 6, the public school my daughter Zoë attended for four years—one of the best public schools in New York City, located in one of the wealthiest neighborhoods. And it's even less likely that she'd end up at the Nightingale-Bamford School for Girls, where Zoë completed her elementary and secondary education. Located in the same neighborhood as P.S. 6, Nightingale is one of the best schools in the country.

The point is that Zoë no more deserves an excellent education than anyone else, nor do children who inherit wealth from their parents deserve more than those who don't. Each of us is a node in a network of practices that skew opportunities and life chances—not only for closely allied nodes (children, friends, neighbors, and so on), but for all other nodes as well. An ethic of gratitude insists that we acknowledge our good fortune and take personally our duty to ensure that good fortune is possible for others as well.

Even though the process of dismantling the consequences of our racist past has barely begun, at least the rhetoric of most religious traditions promotes racial equality, even if many religious institutions fall far short of the goal. When it comes to the environment, however, traditional religions often passively endorse the dominion doctrine, which follows from God's edict to Adam and Eve: "Be fruitful, and multiply, and replenish the earth, and subdue it: and have dominion over the fish of the sea, and over the fowl of the air, and over every living thing that moveth upon the earth" (Genesis 1:28, King James Version). An ethic of gratitude demands that we take personally the sources of sustenance upon which we depend, as well as the larger environment that makes all life possible.

In particular, we need to take more personally the animals and plants that give their lives for our sustenance. Having grown up on a farm, I'm not being sentimental. I know how food happens. But I believe our lack of reverence for the way we grow and prepare our food is killing us, in both body and spirit.

In his book *The Omnivore's Dilemma: A Natural History of Four Meals*, Michael Pollan looks at four meals—a fast-food meal, a meal made from organic ingredients from around the world, a meal made from locally grown ingredients, and a meal Pollan literally hunts and gathers himself—and asks what's on the plate. What did it take to grow or raise the ingredients and get them to the table? And is the meal good—not only good to eat and good for you to eat, but good in ethical terms as well?

In the case of the fast-food meal, what's on the plate (or in the wrapper or the cup) is mostly corn. Laboratory measurements of the meal consumed by Pollan's family of four revealed that corn made up 100 percent of the soda, 65 percent of the salad dressing, 56 percent of the chicken nuggets, 52 percent of the cheeseburger, and 23 percent of the French fries. The cornification of our food system, as Pollan calls it, has degraded our physical health (too many calories, too much processed food, too little diversity) and damaged our environment (too much fertilizer, too many pesticides, too many antibiotics). The decision to eat a fast-food meal sends an instruction to corporate headquarters: keep making food this way, with all the corresponding destruction of the environment, degradation of animals, and damage to our bodies.

At the other end of the spectrum lies the meal Pollan hunts and gathers for himself, which includes wild pig, egg fettuccini with morels, garden salad, and a cherry tart. He didn't open a can of stock to prepare the meal, he said, because "stock doesn't come from a can; it comes from the bones of animals." He admits that there was nothing very realistic about the meal. But once in a while, as a kind of ritual, a meal that is eaten in full consciousness of what it took to make it is worthwhile, "if only as a way to remind us of the true costs of the things we take for granted" (pp. 409–410). Pollan concludes:

> *This is not the way I want to eat every day. I like to be able to open*
> *a can of stock and I like to talk about politics, or the movies, at the*

*dinner table sometimes instead of food. But imagine for a moment if we once again knew, strictly as a manner of course, these few unremarkable things: What it is we're eating. Where it came from. How it found its way to our table. And what, in a true accounting, it really cost. We could then talk about some other things at dinner. For we would no longer need any reminding that however we choose to feed ourselves, we eat by the grace of nature, not industry, and what we're eating is never anything more or less than the body of the world. (p. 411)*

You are eating the body of the world—literally. Put differently, the universe changes in response to whether you have a fast-food hamburger or a local chicken for dinner. It changes in response to whether your blueberries came from a local farm or from South America. Because you need to eat, you owe the universe a debt of gratitude for your sustenance. But also because you need to eat, you're responsible for the kind of universe that gets created to respond to how you meet your need for sustenance.

I recently went to see my primary care physician for my annual physical—my first check-up with her since my previous physician moved to Houston last year. In the course of discussing my somewhat higher than necessary cholesterol levels, I discovered that she has been a vegetarian for twenty-five years and that my previous physician has since turned vegan.

This news gave me pause. I know where saturated fats come from. I also know that we grow enough food on this planet each year to feed 11 billion people. A goodly portion of that food goes to cows, pigs, and chickens, most of which lead lives of brutal desperation until they get eaten. Increasingly, I find myself moving away from habitually eating animals.

Let me suggest several books for further exploration on this topic. In Michael Pollan's book titled *In Defense of Food*, he addresses the question "What *should* we have for dinner?" His answer: "Eat food. Not too much. Mostly plants." Novelist Barbara Kingsolver tells the story in her book *Animal, Vegetable, Miracle* of how her family attempted to feed themselves for a year with food they and their neighbors grew. And if you think the mix of ethics and eating is mainly a sentimental exercise to save suffering chickens and traumatized cabbages, read *The China Study* by Colin and Thomas Campbell. It's not only about chickens, cows, and cabbages; it's also about us.

Another experience we need to take more personally concerns the larger environment upon which all life depends. At our peril, we have run out the string on the biblical command to exercise dominion over the earth and subdue it. An ethic of gratitude demands that we treat our physical environment as the incubus of a fragile and precious gift: life itself. Watch *The Story of Stuff* on YouTube. It will take you fifteen minutes, and it will motivate you to clean out your closets and ask why they got full in the first place.

According to Paul Hawken's book, *Natural Capitalism*, which he co-authored with Amory B. Lovins and L. Hunter Lovins, 99 percent of the total material flow in North America—the stuff we harvest, mine, process, and transport—winds up in a landfill or recycling plant within six months (p. 81). Put differently, only 1 percent of the stuff we make remains in use six months after its sale. Hawken's 1 percent materials efficiency takes into consideration not only end products—food, books, furniture, iPhones, clothes, cars, and so on—but also everything it took to make them: the gloves used by the woman who checked the circuit board on your child's Xbox 360, for example, or the container that held the ink used to print the packaging of your plasma television, or the chainsaw blade used to fell the tree that became the paper in your printer. There's a lot more stuff in our cupboards and closets than meets the eye—nearly a hundred times more stuff, in fact.

I think we as a society have developed an excessive consumptive enthusiasm. The earth and its people have invested a lot of materials, energy, and time in the stuff we buy. As we make buying decisions, we should respect the global efforts that make them possible.

Also, watch the fifteen-part BBC series *Planet Earth*. The first twelve episodes are breathtaking and mesmerizing. But don't neglect the three episodes at the end. They pose two main problems. First, we easily fall in love with pandas and tigers and the like, and we'll spend millions to save them when they are endangered. But life on the planet doesn't rely on pandas; it relies on what the biologist E. O. Wilson calls bugs and weeds. We need to care more about the lower-level forms of life that keep the wheel of life going around. Second, most of the people directly affected by conservation efforts are poor people. We're quick to tell them to quit killing elephants, for example. But what if that's the best way for them to feed their families?

The environmental issue that perhaps most capaciously engages the "take everything personally" mandate of the ethic of gratitude is global warming, an issue that has become perilously easy to ignore, at least for many people. Several years ago, the United Nations published in summary form a report of the Intergovernmental Panel on Climate Change. The report was notable for two reasons. The first is the level of confidence placed in its findings. The six hundred scientists who authored the study state without equivocation that the climate of the earth is changing in very significant ways and will continue to do so for the foreseeable future. They also state that it is "very likely" (meaning they are more than 90 percent certain) that humans are the cause of this climate change.

The second notable feature is that representatives of the sponsoring governments (including the United States, Saudi Arabia, and China) had to agree with the findings and the language of the report before it could be published. Left to their own devices, the scientists would have pegged the likelihood of human cause at more than 95 percent, or extremely likely. Under governmental pressure, the scientists toned down their language from extremely likely to very likely, meaning they are more than 90 percent certain that humans are causing climate change. In either case, when leading scientists and governments agree that bad things are happening to our environment and that, nine chances out of ten, humans are to blame, it's time for decisive action.

So why aren't we doing anything about global warming? John Lanchester, author of *A Debt to Pleasure*, wrote a perceptive review article for the *London Review of Books* about climate change, which he titled "Warmer, Warmer." Lanchester asks why climate change activists have not been more strident and violent in their protests. Is it that they are simply too nice or too educated? "Or is it that even the people who feel most strongly about climate change on some level can't quite bring themselves to believe in it?" he wonders.

Lanchester admits that he finds in himself a strong degree of psychological resistance to the subject of climate change. He says, "I just don't want to think about it.... [I] spent a couple of formative decades trying not to think too much about nuclear war, a subject which offered the same combination of individual impotence and prospective planetary catastrophe. Global warming is even harder to ignore, not so much because it is increasingly omnipresent in the media but because the evidence for it is starting to be manifest in daily life. Even a city boy like me can see that the world is a little warmer than it was." He concludes, "I suspect we're reluctant to think about it because we're worried that if we start we will have no choice but to think about nothing else."

And so we don't think about it. On a spectacularly beautiful day, when the sun is seasonally warm and the flowers are blooming, and the air is fragrant with the smells of spring, it is easy not to think about it. But we must: what we choose not to know can hurt us. Willful ignorance about the human role in climate change threatens not only the future of our planet but, increasingly, its present as well. Remember, it's not only your world; it's you. So take it personally.

The area in which traditional religion has done and continues to do the most damage, ethically speaking, has to do with the status of women. For a long time, Planet Earth has been a dangerous place to be female—and traditional religion has been a persistent source of the danger. The patriarchy that has controlled our social, political, and religious institutions for more than four millennia has massive residual support: a male god, male prophets and messiahs, and male-dominated economic and political institutions. They were designed to endure—whatever the cost.

This male-pattern behavior has evolutionary roots, which scientist and physician Malcolm Potts and journalist Thomas Hayden explore in their book *Sex and War: How Biology Explains Warfare and Terrorism and Offers a Path to a Safer World*. They write, "In a handful of social mammals, a highly specialized behavior has evolved [. . . stretching back 5 to 7 million years or more] in which teams of adults—almost always males—attack and kill individuals of the same species" (p. 11).

In evolutionary terms, male team aggression yielded obvious benefits, such as more territory. "A larger territory meant more resources, more resources meant more females, more females meant the opportunity for more sex, and more sex meant more offspring carrying the male's genes, aggressive tendencies and all, to the next generation. Those males who coordinate their violence in teams became the winners in the ruthless war of nature" (p. 12).

Male team aggression is a Stone Age solution to a Stone Age problem, however. Its goal was to destroy competing males and subdue and impregnate females. The problem is that, in terms of male behavior, the Stone Age has not ended. When men band together, either explicitly or subtly, to keep women down or keep women out—or both—bad things happen.

And bands of men still fight to keep women in the Stone Age. Religious fundamentalists around the world are building alliances to fortify the all-male club and keep women subdued and subordinate. It's true that women's organizations and other civil society initiatives are pushing back, but the patriarchy remains deeply entrenched. Even in the United States, the backlash against women's rights has become well organized and well funded. In order to diminish this Stone Age behavior, we need to dismantle Stone Age institutions.

If we don't, civilization itself will be at risk. Male-pattern behavior kept humanity alive during an era when our species had but a fledgling purchase on this planet. For humanity to survive in the coming era, men will need to recognize that the era of male team aggression has passed. Whether the arena is religion or economics or politics, unless women assume a more-than-equal role in dismantling our fraternal past and building a different kind of future, we are doomed.

Potts and Hayden observe, "For literally millions of years our male ancestors teamed up and went out to kill their neighbors. For many of our mothers, over many hundreds of thousands of generations, the least costly strategy was to go along with the male agenda of team aggression. It's a predisposition that leaves the contemporary world spending 3.3 billion dollars a day on the military, while almost three billion people live on two dollars a day or less." They conclude, "For many, this level of military spending represents a good investment in a dangerous world—until we realize that the world itself need not be so dangerous" (p. 377).

What will it take for the situation to change? It will require the continuing expansion of human rights to ensure that individuals—especially women—realize their right to liberty and equality and that states effectively defend and protect those rights. It will also require the embrace of an ethic of gratitude to ensure that individuals—especially men—use their liberty to pursue worthy purposes. Virtuous men recognize how much they depend on the women around them and how much their own lives are diminished, both morally and practically, when women are subordinated and degraded. And all of us—men and women alike—need to remember that women in degrading situations will need our help to get out. Their freedom is contingent, at least in part, upon us.

I admit that many of these ethical problems appear intractable. The more you learn, the easier it is to lose hope. It's hard to take everything personally and remain optimistic. Remember that engagement is the antidote to despair. Pick something that matters to you. Learn all you can. Get involved, if even in a small way.

Members of my congregation often come to me feeling discouraged about the state of the world. They feel inadequate in the face of problems that confront us and injustices that surround us. "I have two children to put through school," one woman said. "I wish I could go to Haiti and help build schools there, but I can't."

"What can I do to make even a small dent in poverty?" another wondered. "I'm not poor, by most standards, but even if I gave away everything I earn, it wouldn't begin to help solve the problem."

While it may be statistically accurate to say that no one can make a significant difference, it's not true. In fact, the opposite is true. All change happens incrementally—and the increments are exceedingly small: one quantum leap at a time.

A quantum leap, you say? We usually think of quantum leaps as large-scale, epic changes. Not so, says Jacques Barzun in his cultural history of the West, *From Dawn to Decadence*. "A 'quantum leap' is not the great pole vault that jargon assumes from the impressive sound of the words; it happens inside the atom without being detectable" (p. 631).

An electron can orbit only at certain distances from the nucleus. These are called quantum levels, and they are the spherical equivalent of floors in an apartment building. The electron can move between floors, but it can only move one floor at a time. It can whirl around on the first floor, or the second, or the third, but it cannot stop in between floors. For some reason, the elevator doors will not open.

This move from one quantum level to another is called, not surprisingly, a quantum leap. No one knows what makes an electron leap, or why it can only move one quantum level at a time, or why there is no in-between. But we do know that when an electron does make the leap, it is making the smallest change it possibly can. Quantum levels are so named because a quantum is the smallest unit of anything. A quantum leap, therefore, describes the smallest possible change.

Here's the point: huge changes in the physical world are simply the accumulated difference made by an infinite number of small changes. The many become one and are increased by one, as Whitehead said. But over time, the accumulated changes can be astounding: the birth of a star or a baby, the exploding of a bomb or the opening of a flower, the warming of the seas in summer or the chilling of the air in autumn.

The same dynamic holds true in the realm of ethics. Human agency is the point of fulcrum where necessity meets possibility and the past becomes the future. Our goal is to cooperate with the creative process in moving toward an ideal harmony. We promote the creative advance when we make choices that increase the complexity and maximize the reciprocity of experience.

The point of fulcrum for an ethic of gratitude is the point where the capacity to decide (wisdom) and the ability to act (courage) are present. That point appears initially in the human realm and subsequently becomes part of the divine realm. In this sense, you and I are human forms of the divine. The active agency of the divine life emerges through our choices and actions. For this reason, an ethic of gratitude takes human agency with ultimate seriousness. We have the freedom to continually create ourselves and the world, one quantum leap at a time.

## CHAPTER 10

# When We're Satisfied

## *Ultimate Meaning*

R ainer Maria Rilke is considered by many to be the greatest German poet of the twentieth century. About a century ago, Rilke penned a series of ten letters to a young man named Franz Xaver Kappus, who was struggling to find his own identity as a poet and writer. Today, these *Letters to a Young Poet*, as the collection is known, rank among the most famous letters ever written.

The initial letter in the series was prompted by a packet of poems Kappus sent to Rilke, asking if the poems were any good. Rilke responded to the query by acknowledging that, in fact, the poems did not stand on their own merit ("Your verses have no style of their own"). But, Rilke went on to say, the issue is not the quality of the poems, which can be revised or even discarded and begun again. The decisive issue is the character of the poet and the depth of the roots from which the poet draws sustenance.

Rilke said to Kappus, "You are looking outside, and that is what you should most avoid right now. No one can advise you or help you—no one. There is only one thing you should do. Go into yourself. Find out the reason that commands you to write; see whether it has spread its roots into the very depths of your heart" (pp. 5–6).

Rilke's first letter culminated in this now-famous dictum: "I can't give you any advice but this: to go into yourself and see how deep the place is from which your life flows" (p. 9).

Several years ago, my wife, Holly, and I made an overnight trip from Manhattan to Lancaster County, Pennsylvania. Beginning in my mid-teens, I lived in the Lancaster area for a number of years and eventually went to college at Franklin & Marshall, where I majored in classics. Holly and I were on our way to attend a retirement party for the Latin professor who had chaired the Classics Department during my time at F&M. En route, as we meandered through lush Amish and Mennonite farms east of Lancaster, we passed a small Mennonite church out in the country. One of my uncles had once served that congregation as its pastor. During my early twenties, I had been youth minister there for a few years and then acting pastor for a short time.

As we passed the church, Holly noticed that I had grown quiet, then pensive. "How do you feel about being here?" she asked. After a long pause, I replied, "Ambivalent. On the one hand, I feel claustrophobic—like I can't breathe. On the other hand, this is the mine where my gold came from."

The Conservative Mennonites of my upbringing took religion with ultimate seriousness. The disciplines of faith and the practice of religion permeated every aspect of our lives. In George Santayana's way of speaking, religion provided us with a world to live in, a coherent and comprehensive world that shaped everything we did and didn't do. It's a fictional world, in my view; based on everything we've learned about the universe over the past half-dozen centuries, I can no longer embrace the idea of a divine revelation from a supernatural God. Nonetheless, I learned from the Mennonites how to take seriously the imperative to become the kind of person I ought to become.

When people reject the claims of traditional religion, they usually reject as well the need to take religion seriously. Even if they occasionally attend services, they tend to be looking for spiritual enrichment rather than another world to live in. A concert on Thursday evening, dinner with friends on Friday evening, a hike around the lake on Saturday, and an hour of worship on Sunday: a dash of spirituality adds a moral patina to a life that otherwise revolves around individual plans and purposes.

The world of religion, in contrast, is the world of a community. More than anything else, my life as a Mennonite was defined by a clear sense of being part of a community—and of the difference between our community of faith and the rest of the world. I was first and foremost a Mennonite. For the Mennonites of my upbringing, faith is the faith of a community. Personal identity follows from adopting the faith of one's parents and assuming a role conferred by the community. The virtue of this mode of religious community is an unassailable sense of being safe and secure, of belonging to a group no matter what. It also requires allegiance and conformity no matter what.

The religious community of my youth was precisely ordered, like the cornrows and picket fences in a Lancaster landscape. My quarrel with the Mennonites developed when it became clear that my faith and my role were not, in significant measure, mine to choose. Many of my childhood friends were able to accept the religious and personal identities handed down to them. They remained Mennonite, nestled in a community where everyone belonged because everyone conformed. I did not. I wanted the freedom to choose my own religious path. My story is a tale of growing up Mennonite and then leaving the faith of my upbringing in search of a new religious home.

Just as important as what I left behind when I left the Mennonite Church, however, is what I took along with me. My deepest religious roots continue to inform my understanding of what it means to take seriously the imperative to become the kind of people we ought to become.

After a prolonged search, I discovered Unitarian Universalism, a tradition made up of two historically Christian denominations, the Unitarians and the Universalists, which had separated independently from the Christian faith over the past couple of centuries and then merged in 1961. Both Unitarians and Universalists left the Christian fold for the same reason: they held fast to views that Christians considered heresies.

The Unitarians took exception to the Christian belief in the triune God: God as Father, Son, and Holy Ghost. Unitarians quarreled with the Trinitarian formula for two reasons: it wasn't scriptural, and it wasn't reasonable. The scriptural proof often advanced in support of the view that Jesus was divine comes from the Gospel according to John, in which Jesus says that "The Father and I are one" (John 10:30). The latest of the four Gospels (it was finalized between sixty and seventy years after Jesus's death), John shows heavy influence from late first-century efforts to use elements of Greek philosophy to distinguish the Jesus story from competing Jewish and Roman religious alternatives. For this reason, while the Gospel of John may be the most theologically interesting of the four Gospels, most scholars agree that it's the least historically reliable when it comes to the words of Jesus.

As it happens, the congregation I currently serve as senior minister—All Souls Unitarian Church in Manhattan—was founded in the wake of a sermon on precisely this point. In April 1819, a young Unitarian minister named William Ellery Channing was traveling from Boston to Baltimore, where he would deliver the sermon at the ordination of Jared Sparks, one of his protégés. On the way to Baltimore, Channing stopped in New York to visit his sister, Lucy Channing Russel, who invited about forty friends to come to her home and hear Channing speak. Jonathan Goodhue, then one of New York's leading merchants and citizens, was in attendance and wrote the following in his diary:

> *I attended with great satisfaction. [Channing] was in delicate health, and read a Sermon from his seat, but it was an excellent one—on the advantages and disadvantages of life in a great City, full of sound reflections and calculated to excite a train of useful thoughts in the mind, and not to bewilder it with incomprehensible and useless dogmas.* (Kring, Liberals Among the Orthodox, *p. 30)*

Channing went on to Baltimore, where he preached what became the most widely disseminated sermon in America before the Civil War, titled "Unitarian Christianity." In it, Channing argued that the doctrine of the Trinity was both contrary to scripture and incompatible with reason. By the time he came back through New York several weeks later on his way home, Channing's controversial sermon had made him a famous man. Again, he was invited to preach, but this time the Russel parlor was far too small. The hall at the College of Physicians and Surgeons was rented—it was the largest hall in New York at the time—and Channing preached three services there, at 10:30 a.m., 3:30 p.m., and 7:30 p.m. Even so, hundreds of people were reportedly turned away at each service for lack of space. A report of the day notes:

> *So great an interest was evidenced by the services of the 16th of May, that it was determined to call a meeting to consult upon measures for securing a suitable place for public worship, where the privilege of hearing preaching of the same character might be enjoyed whenever opportunity offered. (Kring, p. 34)*

About six months later, on November 15, 1819, the First Congregational Church of New York was officially incorporated (Unitarian was not an option under then-current New York State religious incorporation laws), with thirty-four founding members. At the dedication of the congregation's new sanctuary in 1821, the preacher, the Rev. Edward Everett, warned:

> *You are dedicating a place of worship to the support of views of revealed truth [which are] different, in some important points, from those of the respectable community in which you live; not extensively understood by your neighbors.... Under these circumstances, it is impossible that you should not be the objects of prejudices, of the unfavorable opinions, of the opposition, with which whatever is new is apt to be regarded. (Kring, pp. 86–87)*

"Whatever is new," in this case, was the not-so-new idea that reason should trump scripture.

The Universalists—the other half of the merger—defined them-selves in a similar way over the doctrine of predestination, which is the idea that God (as traditionally understood) decided the fate of indi-vidual human beings before he created the world. In particular, the Universalists abhorred the idea that a loving God would damn certain people to hell before he even created them. Such a doctrine made no sense, nor was it biblical. Like the Unitarians, the Universalists cham-pioned Enlightenment values. They believed that the universe can be understood through the use of reason, that experience is the basis of human understanding, and that history is largely a history of progress.

After a prolonged search, I was relieved and delighted to discover Unitarian Universalism. Like the Mennonites, Unitarian Universalists labor tirelessly to relieve human suffering, advance justice, and make this world a better place. At the Universalist Convention in 1790, the Universalists became the first denomination in America to call for the abolition of slavery. A month after the historic meeting at Seneca Falls, New York, in 1848 sparked the women's rights movement, key national women's suffrage leaders convened a follow-up Women's Rights Convention at the Unitarian Church in Rochester, New York, to plan strategy. The Unitarian Universalist Service Committee was formed in the wake of Unitarian-led efforts to rescue Jews bound for Hitler's death camps. One of my ministerial colleagues at All Souls, the Rev. Richard Leonard, marched with Dr. Martin Luther King Jr. at Selma, as did a number of other Unitarian Universalist ministers and lay people. One of their number, James Reeb, was bludgeoned during the melee in Selma and died several days later. Social justice stands at the very center of the Unitarian Universalist commitment to the larger community and the world.

When it comes to religious identity, however, Mennonites and Unitarian Universalists stand at opposite poles. Unlike the faith of my upbringing, this newfound tradition insists on the complete freedom of the individual in matters of faith and practice.

This insight makes Unitarian Universalism an excessively modern approach to religion. Charles Taylor writes in his book *The Ethics of Authenticity* that "individualism names what many people consider to be the finest achievement of modern civilization." He continues: "We live in a world where people have a right to choose for themselves their own pattern of life, to decide in conscience what convictions to espouse, to determine the shape of their lives in a whole host of ways that their ancestors couldn't control" (p. 2).

On these terms, Unitarian Universalism unites individualism and a spiritual sensibility. What is wrong with that, you may ask? Nothing at all, so long as our commitment to individualism is properly construed. But often it is not. A commitment to individualism can foster two destructive impulses: first, a wrongheaded belief that community is fundamentally coercive; and second, a misguided belief that individuals are most self-fulfilled when they are most autonomous.

Make no mistake: these are powerfully seductive impulses. I know well how coercive a community of any kind can be, especially a community of faith. The Amish, first cousins to the Mennonites, literally ban from their family and community life those who are unwilling to accept the dictates of the group's common identity. If one wants to be part of us, they say, then one must look like us and act like us and believe like us. In light of such situations, it is easy to conclude that community is fundamentally coercive, and that astute individuals should gather to form not communities (in the traditional sense) but coalitions—groups of people who pursue a common goal only because it happens to coincide with each of their individual goals.

The second impulse, the one that drives toward individual autonomy, is equally seductive. The life mandate that follows from Descartes's discovery that "I think, therefore I am" can be expressed with equal simplicity: "Know thyself" or "To thine own self be true." In other words, we each have the right to shape our individual lives, grounded in our own sense of what is really important or valuable.

If this individual-centered approach becomes a moral absolute, then we have nothing in common save a moral obligation to leave each other alone when it comes to anything that matters. We have a moral duty not to challenge each other's values. We cannot confront each other about whether or not there are values we ought to hold or ways of life we should pursue. Religious community becomes impossible.

As Charles Taylor notes, "the dark side of individualism is a centering on the self, which both flattens and narrows our lives, makes them poorer in meaning, and less concerned with others or society" (p. 4). This face of individualism leaves me most isolated as a person precisely in those parts of my life that should be most productive of meaning. This is a specter I am simply not willing to abide. I may be an individual, but I do not want to live my life as an island.

The truth is that we form our individual identities not by breaking our ties with everyone and everything, but by virtue of those ties. I am who I am by virtue of my relationships with others. A community of faith is not peripheral to our individual quests for meaning and purpose. In a real sense, our relationships with others create the possibility of becoming who we ought to become in the first place.

Our existential situation is that we are utterly dependent on the people and the world around us, yet we often live our lives as if we are not. The experience of worship within a community of faith helps save us from this sin of separation by instilling within us a discipline of gratitude—a sense of our connection to and dependence upon everything: all that is present in our world and universe, as well as all that is past and all that is possible. Our commitment to others within our community models the ethic of gratitude that ultimately characterizes our commitment to everyone and everything.

If the individualist approach to religion gets pushed to its logical extreme, you get the approach Alain de Botton espouses in *Religion for Atheists: A Non-Believer's Guide to the Uses of Religion*. As I noted in chapter six, Botton insists that the claims of religion are entirely false, yet he readily agrees that religions have important things to teach the secular world.

When Botton looks at the various elements of religious practice and asks which ones might be useful, he's headed in the right direction but stops short of the goal. Religion includes good art and great architecture and stirring music and instructive stories and comforting rituals and prophetic challenges. But until they all fit together in a way that unites spiritual need and moral imagination, they don't add up to transformed lives and a changed world. Religion is an all-or-nothing experience, like Beethoven's Ninth. Religion happens—and transformation comes—when a community of people practices faith together.

In January 2012, I visited Israel with an interfaith group of clergy from New York City. We spent some time with Natan Sharansky, the Russian mathematician and chess champion who became a human rights activist after the Soviets refused his application to emigrate to Israel. You may recall the image of Sharansky in 1986 walking across the bridge in Berlin after nine years in a Siberian prison.

Still a vital force in Israeli politics today, Sharansky told us that the most profound realization of his life came to him in prison; all of his experience since has substantiated this insight. People want two things, he said: they want to be free and they want to belong. These are the two human passions: freedom and identity. The discovery of your identity, he said, gives you the strength to fight for both your own freedom and the freedom of others. He insisted that identity comes first: until you know who you are and where you belong, you can never be free.

This is a counterintuitive claim. Most of the time, we think of freedom in terms of absence: no obligations, no constraints, and no commitments. In that spirit, I could say: you are now free to perform Beethoven's Ninth Symphony. Nothing is holding you back. But wait, you quickly say, I need a cello and a decade of lessons, along with a hundred other instrumentalists and fifty singers, not to mention a conductor and lots of rehearsal time. Until I'm part of a symphony orchestra, I'm not free to perform Beethoven's Ninth Symphony.

Until you find a place to belong, you can never be free. This same principle applies to sports. You aren't free to play unless you belong to one of the teams. It also applies to politics. The collection of shared intentions and actions we call government is the prerequisite of our freedom as Americans, not the obstacle to it. Discovering where you belong is the first step toward being set free.

I spend time every week with members and friends of All Souls who entered our doors in bondage—captive to a lonely spirit or a worried mind, a pernicious addiction or a destructive relationship, a lost sense of meaning or a vanished sense of purpose. Again and again, they tell me that the sense of identity and belonging they discovered at All Souls has given them the freedom to make a change for the better. Freedom is another word for everything yet to gain.

At its best, All Souls provides a temple of belonging and freedom. Our shared faith—our collective leap of moral imagination—imagines a better character within each of us and a better world for all of us. This faith is buoyed by a God we can believe in—a God of possibility and promise—and it is sustained by our presence together in worship, where we practice our religion. In this temple, we can find ourselves and be set free.

My goal in writing this book has not been to hold up All Souls as a model modern congregation or Unitarian Universalism as the model modern religion. While most Unitarian Universalists have left behind the idea of a supernatural God, many have also left behind the idea of religion—the idea that a community of faith must be defined by a coherent and comprehensive set of theological commitments and religious practices held in common. Many Unitarian Universalist congregations operate in the mode of Botton's wistful non-believer, using elements from various established traditions to provide spiritual edification and moral guidance for each individual seeker.

Even so, I hope that Unitarian Universalism can somehow eventually fulfill its promise. Diana Eck, a professor of religion at Harvard and one of the world's leading scholars of religion, preached the sermon at my installation as senior minister of All Souls. On that occasion, she spoke about the congregation All Souls aspires to be and the difference Unitarian Universalists aspire to make.

> *If there ever were a time that we need to spin out a new fabric of belonging and a wider sense of "we" for the human community, it is certainly now. . . . Developing a consciousness of our growing religious inter-relatedness, developing a moral compass that will give us guidance in the years ahead—these are certainly among the most important tasks of our time. . . . You have a theological orientation toward the oneness and mystery of God that is essential for the world of religious difference in which we live. . . . You are, in my estimation, the church of the new millennium. In this era, Unitarian Universalism is not the lowest common denominator, but the highest common calling.*

Even if her aspiration eventually turns out to be true for Unitarian Universalism, it must also become true more broadly. In religious terms, I am convinced that what the world needs now is a way of being religious for people who take both faith and reason seriously. The world needs a religion for children of the Enlightenment, in other words. As of yet, however, no one has put all the pieces together, orchestrating the religious equivalent of a modern-day Beethoven's Ninth Symphony.

In the meantime, we need to take everything we know into account as we decide what to believe and how to live. The decision to transform your life by changing how you think and act takes courage. As you take the first steps, look around for a like-minded congregation to share the journey—a place where you can belong. This may be difficult: the religious landscape in our nation is dominated by communities that define themselves by outmoded beliefs, as well as by individuals who embrace a solitary spirituality—or no spirituality at all. None of these approaches will yield ultimate meaning, however, which is why a satisfying faith requires a journey.

If Americans are telling pollsters the truth, however, you have lots of company. Tens of millions of spiritual seekers—both within the religions of the book and outside the fold—long to reconcile the discoveries of science, the wisdom of religion, and the meaning of life. The adventure of faith requires the ultimate commitment, but it can lead to ultimate meaning. You can find yourself in the place where you belong and, in so doing, be set free.

# Bibliography

Alter, Robert. *The Five Books of Moses: A Translation with Commentary.* New York: W.W. Norton, 2004.

Anselm. *Proslogion, with the Replies of Gaunilo and Anselm.* Translated, with introduction and notes, by Thomas Williams. Indianapolis: Hackett Publishing Company, 1995.

Aquinas, Thomas. *Summa Theologiae: Volume 1, The Existence of God, Part 1: Questions 1-13.* Garden City, NY: Image Books, 1969.

Aristotle. *Metaphysics.* Translated by Hugh Tredennick. Cambridge, MA, and London: Harvard University Press, 1933.

———. *Nicomachean Ethics.* Translated by H. Rackham. Cambridge, MA, and London: Harvard University Press, 1934.

Armstrong, Karen. *A History of God: The 4,000-Year Quest of Judaism, Christianity, and Islam.* New York: Ballantine Books, 1993.

Arnold, Matthew. *Poems.* Edited by Miriam Allott. Oxford and New York: Oxford University Press, 1995.

Augustine. *The Confessions of St. Augustine.* New York: Grosset & Dunlap, 1950.

———. *Tractates on the Gospel of John 1-10 (The Fathers of the Church, Volume 78).* Washington, DC: Catholic University of America Press, 2000.

Barzun, Jacques. *From Dawn to Decadence: 500 Years of Western Cultural Life; 1500 to the Present.* New York: HarperCollins, 2000.

Blackburn, Simon. *Being Good: A Short Introduction to Ethics.* Oxford: Oxford University Press, 2001.

———. *Think: A Compelling Introduction to Philosophy.* Oxford: Oxford University Press, 1999.

Bonhoeffer, Dietrich. *The Cost of Discipleship,* rev. ed. Translated by R. H. Fuller. New York: Macmillan, 1959.

Braght, Thieleman J. van. *The Bloody Theater or Martyrs Mirror of the Defenseless Christians Who Baptized Only Upon Confession of Faith, and Who Suffered and Died for the Testimony of Jesus, Their Saviour, From the Time of Christ to the Year A.D. 1660.* Translated by Joseph F. Sohm. Scottdale, PA: Mennonite Publishing House, 1938.

Campbell, T. Colin, and Thomas M. Campbell. *The China Study.* Dallas: BenBella Books, 2006.

Camus, Albert. *The Myth of Sisyphus and Other Essays.* Translated by Justin O'Brien. New York: Vintage Books, 1991.

———. *Resistance, Rebellion, and Death*. Translated by Justin O'Brien. New York: Modern Library, 1960.

Cizmar, Paula, Catherine Filloux, Gail Kriegel, Carol K. Mack, Ruth Margraff, Anna Deavere Smith, and Susan Yankowitz. *SEVEN*. New York: Dramatists Play Service, 2009.

Coller, Barry S. "The Physician-scientist, the State, and the Oath: Thoughts for Our Time." *The Journal of Clinical Investigation* 116, no. 10 (October 2006): 2567–2570.

Cone, James H. *God of the Oppressed*. New York: Seabury Press, 1975.

Coogan, Michael D., ed. *The New Oxford Annotated Bible, Third Edition (New Revised Standard Version)*. Oxford and New York: Oxford University Press, 2001.

Culotta, Elizabeth. "On the Origin of Religion." *Science* 326 (November 6, 2009): 784–787.

Daly, Mary. *Beyond God the Father: Toward a Philosophy of Women's Liberation*. Boston: Beacon Press, 1973.

Danchin, Antoine. *The Delphic Boat: What Genomes Tell Us*. Translated by Alison Quayle. Cambridge, MA: Harvard University Press, 2003.

Dawkins, Richard. *The God Delusion*. Boston and New York: Houghton Mifflin, 2006.

de Botton, Alain. *Religion for Atheists: A Non-Believer's Guide to the Uses of Religion*. New York: Pantheon, 2012.

Descartes, René. *Meditations on First Philosophy: With Selections from the Objections and Replies*. Translated and edited by John Cottingham. Cambridge: Cambridge University Press, 1996.

Dewey, John. *A Common Faith*. New Haven: Yale University Press, 1991.

Dickens, Charles. *A Christmas Carol*. London: Barnes & Noble Books, 1994.

Dickinson, Emily. *The Complete Poems of Emily Dickinson*. Boston: Little, Brown, 1960.

Duffy, Eamon. "Early Christian Impresarios." *New York Review of Books* (March 29, 2007).

Dunn, Stephen. *New and Selected Poems 1979–1994*. New York: W.W. Norton, 1995.

Dyson, Freeman J. *Disturbing the Universe*. New York: Basic Books, 1979.

Ehrman, Bart. *Forged: Writing in the Name of God—Why the Bible's Authors Are Not Who We Think They Are*. San Francisco: HarperOne, 2012.

———. *Truth and Fiction in "The Da Vinci Code": A Historian Reveals What We Really Know about Jesus, Mary Magdalene, and Constantine*. Oxford: Oxford University Press, 2006.

Emerson, Ralph Waldo. *Essays and Poems*. New York: Library of America, 1996.

Fay, Martha. *Do Children Need Religion? How Parents Today Are Thinking about the Big Questions*. New York: Pantheon, 1993.

Ferris, Timothy. *Seeing in the Dark*. New York: Simon & Schuster, 2002.

Feuerbach, Ludwig. *The Essence of Christianity*. Translated by George Eliot. Amherst, NY: Prometheus Books, 1989.

Foot, Philippa. "The Problem of Abortion and the Doctrine of Double Effect." *Oxford Review* 5 (1967): 5–15.

Frankl, Viktor E. *Man's Search for Meaning: An Introduction to Logotherapy*. Translated by Ilse Lasch. Boston: Beacon Press, 1959.

Greene, Brian. *The Fabric of the Cosmos: Space, Time, and the Texture of Reality*. New York: Alfred A. Knopf, 2004.

Guengerich, L. Glen. *Our Goodly Heritage*. Kalona, IA: East Union Mennonite Church, 1984.

Hardy, Thomas. *Jude the Obscure*. Oxford: Oxford University Press, 1985.

Hawken, Paul, Amory B. Lovins, and L. Hunter Lovins. *Natural Capitalism: Creating the Next Industrial Revolution*. Boston: Back Bay Books, 2000.

Hildegard. *Hildegard of Bingen: Selected Writings*. Translated by Mark Atherton. London: Penguin Books, 2001.

Hoving, Thomas. *Greatest Works of Art of Western Civilization*. New York: Artisan, 1997.

James, William. *The Varieties of Religious Experience*. New York: Collier Books, 1961.

Jordan, Judith V., Alexandra G. Kaplan, Jean Baker Miller, Irene P. Stiver, and Janet L. Surrey. *Women's Growth in Connection: Writings from the Stone Center*. New York and London: Guilford Press, 1991.

Joyce, Kathryn. *Quiverfull: Inside the Christian Patriarchy Movement*. Boston: Beacon Press, 2009.

Karahasan, Dževad. "A Mockery Out of Maastricht." *Guardian* (July 8, 1993): 8.

King, Martin Luther, Jr. *A Testament of Hope: The Essential Writings and Speeches of Martin Luther King, Jr.* Edited by James M. Washington. San Francisco: Harper & Row, 1986.

Kingsolver, Barbara. *Animal, Vegetable, Miracle: A Year of Food Life*. New York: HarperCollins, 2007.

Kring, Walter Donald. *Henry Whitney Bellows*. Boston: Skinner House, 1979.

———. *Liberals among the Orthodox: Unitarian Beginnings in New York City, 1819–1839*. Boston: Beacon Press, 1974.

Kristof, Nicholas, and Cheryl WuDunn. *Half the Sky: Turning Oppression into Opportunity for Women Worldwide*. New York: Alfred A. Knopf, 2009.

Lanchester, John. "Warmer, Warmer." *London Review of Books* 29, no. 6 (March 22, 2007): 3–9.

Langewiesche, William. *Fly by Wire: The Geese, the Glide, the Miracle on the Hudson*. New York: Macmillan, 2009.

Lerner, Gerda. *The Creation of Patriarchy*. New York and Oxford: Oxford University Press, 1986.

Lipsitz, George. *How Racism Takes Place*. Philadelphia: Temple University Press, 2011.

Lorde, Audre. "Uses of the Erotic: The Erotic as Power." In *Sister Outsider: Essays and Speeches*. Freedom, CA: Crossing Press, 1984.

Merrin, Jeredith. *Bat Ode*. Chicago: University of Chicago Press, 2001.

Muller, Wayne. *Sabbath: Finding Rest, Renewal, and Delight in Our Busy Lives*. New York: Bantam Books, 1999.

Nagel, Thomas. *What Does It All Mean? A Very Short Introduction to Philosophy*. New York and Oxford: Oxford University Press, 1987.

Nussbaum, Martha C. "Disabled Lives: Who Cares?" *New York Review of Books* (January 11, 2001).

———. "Four Paradigms of Philosophical Politics." *The Monist* 83, no. 4 (October 2000): 465–490.

———. *The Fragility of Goodness: Luck and Ethics in Greek Tragedy and Philosophy*. Cambridge: Cambridge University Press, 1986.

Olson, Theodore B. "The Conservative Case for Gay Marriage." *Newsweek* (January 8, 2010).

Pagels, Elaine. *Adam, Eve, and the Serpent*. New York: Random House, 1988.

Peterson, Christopher, and Martin E. P. Seligman. *Character Strengths and Virtues: A Handbook and Classification*. Oxford: Oxford University Press, 2004.

Plato. *Cratylus, Parmendies, Greater Hippias, Lesser Hippias*. Translated by Harold North Fowler. Cambridge, MA, and London: Harvard University Press, 1926.

———. *Laches, Protagoras, Meno, Euthydemus*. Translated by W. R. M. Lamb. Cambridge, MA, and London: Harvard University Press, 1924.

Pollan, Michael. *In Defense of Food: An Eater's Manifesto*. New York: Penguin Press, 2008.

———. *The Omnivore's Dilemma: A Natural History of Four Meals*. New York: Penguin Press, 2006.

Potts, Malcolm, and Thomas Hayden. *Sex and War: How Biology Explains Warfare and Terrorism and Offers a Path to a Safer World*. Dallas: BenBella Books, 2008.

Quine, W. V. *From A Logical Point of View*. New York: Harper & Row, 1963.

Rawls, John. *A Theory of Justice*. Oxford: Oxford University Press, 1971.

Richardson, Robert D. *William James: In the Maelstrom of American Modernism*. Boston and New York: Houghton Mifflin, 2006.

Rilke, Rainer Maria. *Letters to A Young Poet*. Translated by Stephen Mitchell. New York: Random House, 1984.

Robinson, Marilynne. "Hysterical Scientism: The Ecstasy of Richard Dawkins." *Harper's Magazine* (November 2006): 83–88.

Santayana, George. *Reason in Religion*. Vol. 3 of *The Life of Reason; or The Phases of Human Progress*. New York: Dover, 1982.

Scarry, Elaine. *On Beauty and Being Just*. Princeton: Princeton University Press, 1999.

Schleiermacher, Friedrich. *The Christian Faith*. Translated by H. R. Mackintosh and J. S. Stewart. Edinburgh: T. & T. Clark, 1928.

———. *On Religion: Speeches to Its Cultured Despisers*. Edited by Richard Crouter. Cambridge: Cambridge University Press, 1988.

Schmidt, Leigh Eric. *Restless Souls: The Making of American Spirituality from Emerson to Oprah*. San Francisco: HarperSanFrancisco, 2005.

Sophocles. *Philoctetes*. Translated by Hugh Lloyd-Jones. Cambridge, MA, and London: Harvard University Press, 1994.

Strand, Mark. *Man and Camel: Poems*. New York: Alfred A. Knopf, 2006.

Suchocki, Marjorie. "Weaving the World." *Process Studies* 14, no. 2 (Summer 1985): 76–86.

Sun Tzu. *The Art of War*. Translated by Lionel Giles. Richmond Hill, Ontario: Prohyptikon Publishing, 2009.

Taylor, Charles. *The Ethics of Authenticity*. Cambridge, MA: Harvard University Press, 1992.

———. *A Secular Age*. Cambridge, MA, and London: Belknap Press of Harvard University Press, 2007.

Taylor, Richard. *Virtue Ethics: An Introduction*. New York: Prometheus Books, 2002.

Thomson, Judith Jarvis. "The Trolley Problem." *Yale Law Journal* 94 (1985): 1395–1415.

Tillich, Paul. *The Courage to Be*. New Haven: Yale University Press, 1952.

Toews, Miriam. *A Complicated Kindness: A Novel*. New York: Counterpoint, 2004.

Wallace, David Foster. *This Is Water: Some Thoughts, Delivered on a Significant Occasion, about Living a Compassionate Life*. New York: Little, Brown, 2009.

Weiner, Eric. "Americans: Undecided About God?" *The New York Times* (December 10, 2011).

———. *Man Seeks God: My Flirtations with the Divine*. New York and Boston: Twelve, 2011.

Whitehead, Alfred North. *Adventures of Ideas*. New York: Free Press, 1967.

———. *The Aims of Education and Other Essays*. New York: Free Press, 1967.

———. *Essays in Science and Philosophy*. New York: Philosophical Library, 1947.

———. *Modes of Thought*. New York: Free Press, 1968.

———. *Process and Reality*, corrected ed. Edited by David Ray Griffin and Donald W. Sherburne. New York: Free Press, 1979.

————. *Religion in the Making.* New York: New American Library, 1974.

————. *Science and the Modern World.* New York: Macmillan, 1948.

Whitman, Walt. *Leaves of Grass: First and "Death-bed" Editions.* With an introduction and notes by Karen Karbiener. New York: Barnes & Noble Classics, 2004.

Wittgenstein, Ludwig. *Philosophical Investigations.* Oxford: Basil Blackwell, 1958.

————. *Tractatus Logico-Philosophicus.* Translated by C. K. Ogden. New York: Cosimo Classics, 2007.

Zolberg, Aristide R. *A Nation by Design: Immigration Policy in the Fashioning of America.* Cambridge, MA: Harvard University Press, 2008.

# Index